THE COOK-ZEN
Wagashi Cookbook

THE COOK-ZEN
Wagashi Cookbook

Traditional Japanese Sweets
Made Simply in the Microwave

By Machiko Chiba

LAKE ISLE PRESS | NEW YORK

Recipes copyright © 2017 by Machiko Chiba

MC MACHIKO ® and COOK-ZEN ® are registered trademarks of
Machiko Cooking USA, Inc.

First published in Japan by Nikkei BP Consulting (http://consult.nikkeibp.co.jp);
first edition, 2009; second edition (revised), 2013.

Photography credits: See page 141

Published in the U.S. by Lake Isle Press, Inc., 2095 Broadway, Suite 301,
New York, NY 10023, (212) 273-0796, e-mail: info@lakeislepress.com

Distributed in the U.S. by National Book Network, Inc., 4501 Forbes Boulevard,
Suite 200, Lanham, MD 20706,1(800) 462-6420, www.nbnbooks.com

Library of Congress Control Number: 2017942379

ISBN-13: 978-1-891105-62-3
ISBN-10: 1-891105-62-0

Editor: Jeanne Hodesh
Book and cover design (U.S. edition): Liz Trovato
Translation: Yuri Funabiki, Akiko Chiba
Food styling: Machiko Chiba

This book is available at special sales discounts for bulk purchases as premiums or
special editions, including customized covers. For more information, contact the
publisher at (212) 273-0796 or by e-mail, info@lakeislepress.com

First U.S edition
Printed in China

10 9 8 7 6 5 4 3 2 1

To my dear mother, Haruko Sato,
who showed me that the most important
ingredient in a recipe is love.

Contents

Making Traditional Japanese Sweets (*Wagashi*) with the Cook-Zen

Traditional Japanese sweets known as *wagashi* are centuries old. The early simple snacks originated in China, but it was in Kyoto, the capital of ancient Japan, that *wagashi*-making became a form of art. At the time, these beautifully crafted sweets were luxury items prepared for nobility. Today, *wagashi* are popular with everyone, though master chefs still train for decades to learn how to create these confections. Given this rich history, it seemed to me that a *wagashi* recipe book would be a wonderful way to share Japan's culinary traditions with the world.

You will see that the color, shape, texture, and flavor of *wagashi* are inspired by Japanese aesthetics, our appreciation of nature (*wabi-sabi*), and the four seasons of the year. Many of the ingredients called for in these recipes are plant-based. Red beans (*azuki*) and white beans (*shiro-azuki* and *shiro-ingen*) are commonly used to make sweet bean paste (*an*). Agar-agar (*kanten*), a seaweed extract that is low in calories and extremely high in fiber, is used to make sweet jelly (*yokan*). Refined Japanese sugar (*wasanbon*) and other rice-based ingredients such as cooked and dried glutinous rice powder (*kanbaiko*), also feature heavily. These ingredients, native to Japan, are part of our cultural heritage.

Made the traditional way, by master chefs, *wagashi* can be time-consuming and difficult to prepare. But with the Cook-Zen microwave pot and the recipes in this book, it's possible to make picture-perfect sweets in minutes. What's more, you'll find that the Cook-Zen brings out the natural flavors of the ingredients, making it possible to use less sugar.

I've also developed plastic *wagashi* molds and tools that, compared to the traditional wooden ones used by professionals, are easy to use and affordable. My line of molds features seasonal shapes, including a Japanese maple leaf (*momiji*), cherry blossom (*sakura*) and Japanese gourd (*hyotan*), which are very common for sweet bean paste (*nerikiri*) desserts. The *wagashi* tool set also includes a tamis for puréeing, push molds for making bean-paste desserts, rectangular molds for agar-agar jelly desserts (*yokan*), and molds for traditional Japanese tea ceremony sweets (*higashi*). For a full list, see pages 20-21. With the Cook-Zen microwave pot and these easy-to-use tools, *wagashi*-making is simple and fun for everyone. I hope you will enjoy these recipes with your family and friends.

6 Good Reasons to Use the Cook-Zen

1. It's healthy.
The Cook-Zen cooks ingredients with little or no water, which means valuable vitamins and nutrients that would normally drain off are retained. And because microwave-cooking times are extremely short, more of these nutrients are preserved. Cook-Zen recipes require very little oil, for a naturally low-fat meal.

2. It's easy.
Cook-Zen recipes feature minimal ingredients that are easy to prepare. Once the pot is in the microwave, there's no need to watch over it or stir it constantly.

3. It's fast.
The Cook-Zen works like a pressure cooker, heating foods evenly and quickly. Most of the recipes take under 10 minutes to prepare.

4. It's delicious.
Ingredients cook with little or no added water in the Cook-Zen, which brings out their natural flavors. Meat and fish dishes are tender and juicy, and vegetables retain their vibrant color and crispness.

5. It's safe.
Microwave cooking is perfect for teenagers and the elderly. You'll never have to worry about the risk of fire from leaving a pot or an open flame unattended.

6. It's environmentally friendly.
Microwave cooking uses less water and generates fewer CO_2 emissions than traditional gas-stove cooking. With shorter cooking times in an energy-efficient microwave, you also save on electricity use.

Cook-Zen Parts

1

1. Top Lid
The top lid has two locks that secure all of the Cook-Zen parts together. Always close these locks before cooking.

2

2. Middle Lid
The middle lid has patented adjustable steam holes that control whether steam is released or contained during cooking. Trapping steam in the Cook-Zen is what makes ingredients cook faster. When cooking rice recipes, we suggest setting the steam holes to "open." For other dishes, the steam holes should be set to "close."

3

3. Sieve
Use this sieve to rinse or drain ingredients. The sieve should not be left in the Cook-Zen when cooking.

4

4. Pot
The Cook-Zen pot is made of thick polypropylene (BPA-free), a material that heats food evenly as it cooks. The pot can also function as a mixing bowl when you are preparing your ingredients.

5

5. Measuring Cup
The Cook-Zen measuring cup has a capacity of 200g (7 fluid ounces).

Calibrating Your Microwave

There are many different types of microwaves on the market, with power wattages ranging from 500 to over 1000 watts. All of the recipes in this book were tested at 600 watts. You can adjust the wattage of your microwave by changing the power level, which represents a percentage of the total wattage. For example, if you have a 1,000-watt microwave, a power level of 6 (or 60%) will lower the wattage to 600. Some microwaves have settings such as "medium" that correspond to specific percentages. While wattage is important, if you should have a 700W microwave, there is no need to lower it to 600W.

As with all methods of cooking, you will have to experiment with the Cook-Zen and your microwave to get an idea of how quickly things cook. In my own experience, even microwaves of the same model and brand name yield slightly different results. If you are new to microwave cooking, it's better to err on the side of undercooking something, as you can always pop it back in the microwave for more time. Also keep in mind that continuous use of a microwave without a break can lead to a build up of heat in the machine. If this is the case, allow it to cool down, or shorten the cooking time.

5 Important Tips

1. Use dry tools:
Bowls, whisks, cutting boards, rolling pins, and other equipment should be completely dry before use. Any moisture on the tools will make it hard to knead and spread flour-based ingredients. It will also make it difficult to whip air into eggs and cream.

2. Keep the bean paste (*an*) moist.
When working with bean paste, make sure your hands are moist but not too wet. Keep a moist cotton cloth or cheesecloth nearby and use it to moisten your hands as needed.

3. Work quickly and carefully.
When kneading, mixing, or working with dough, do it quickly and efficiently.

4. Follow the recipe exactly as written.
Sifting and straining, the simplest steps, are the most important. Do not omit any steps. It will affect the final result.

5. Less is more.
A little bit of food coloring goes a long way, so be careful when adding it to your desserts. Remember, once you add coloring you cannot take it out.

The Wagashi Pantry: Essential Ingredients

Bean Pastes (*An*)

1. Red Bean Powder (*Koshian Powder*)

Red bean powder is made from red beans that have been cooked, made into a paste, and then freeze-dried and ground into a powder. It is unsweetened. Combined with sugar and water, it is used to make sweet bean paste (*an*).

2. Navy Bean or White Bean Powder (*Shiroan Powder*)

White bean powder is used in the same way as red bean powder (described above).

Sugars

3. Refined White Sugar (*Jyohakutou*)

This is the most commonly used sugar in Japanese desserts and cooking in general. The granules are fine, with a semi-moist texture.

4. Caster Sugar (*Guranyutou*)

Caster sugar has a very fine grain, much smaller than refined white sugar (*jyohakutou*). Internationally, it is the most commonly used type.

 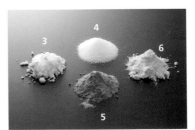

5. Raw Japanese Black Sugar (*Kurozatou* or *Kokutou*)

Raw black sugar is made from sugar cane and/or sugar beets from the Amami Islands in Okinawa, Japan. Because it is minimally processed, it retains most of its vitamins and minerals and has a unique aroma similar to brown sugar.

6. Refined Japanese Sugar (*Wasanbon*)

This is a fine-grained sugar made from a variety of sugar cane called *taketoh*. This fine, powder-like sugar, which melts in your mouth, is ideal for Japanese *wagashi*. *Wasanbon* is made locally in the Tokushima and Kagawa prefectures of Shikoku.

Agar-Agar and Gelatin

7. Stick Agar-Agar and String Agar-Agar

Agar-agar (*kanten*) is a gelatinous substance extracted from seaweed and sea kelp, first discovered in the Edo period (1603-1868). In Japan, the prefectures of Nagano and Gifu are known for agar-agar production. The recipes in this book call for the stick form.

8. Sheet Gelatin and Powdered Gelatin

Gelatin is dried collagen derived from animal by-products, namely, beef and pork skin, bones, and tendons. It is used in chilled jelly desserts.

Flours and Starches

Plant-based starches are an important part of the *wagashi* pantry, and rice flours, in particular, play a key role. Two types of rice are used (glutinous rice—also called sweet rice or *mochi* rice—and regular Japanese short-grain rice) to make a variety of rice flours that differ in how they are processed. Before being milled into flour, the rice may be steamed and dried, baked, or soaked in water. The granulation of the flour can also vary from very fine to coarse. The number of processing techniques shows how creative the Japanese are with ingredients. Different types of rice flour yield different textures, so it's important to use the specific kind called for in recipes.

Bean flours and starch extracted from the roots of plants are also staple *wagashi* ingredients, reflecting the importance of natural ingredients in Japanese sweets.

1. Mochiko

Uncooked sweet *mochi* rice is washed, dried, and milled into flour. *Mochiko* is often labeled as "sweet rice flour" or "glutinous rice." Commonly used to make Sweet Mochi Rice Balls (*Ohagi*, page 64) and Big Fortune Rice Cakes (*Daifuku Mochi*, page 68).

2. Domyojiko

Sweet *mochi* rice is steam-cooked, dried, then coarsely ground. Used to make Cherry Blossom Rice Cakes (*Domyoji Sakura Mochi*, page 60) and Camellia Rice Cakes (*Tsubaki Mochi*, page 62).

3. Jyoshinko

Uncooked, short-grain rice is washed and milled into a fine powder. Once the flour is combined with hot water, the texture becomes thick and elastic. Used to make Skewered Rice Cakes (*Mitarashi Dango*, page 67).

4. Shiratamako

Sweet *mochi* rice is soaked, then milled in water. The liquid and its fine rice powder is strained through a sieve, then dried. Once cooked, its soft, elastic texture is favored to make Edamame Rice Cakes (*Zunda Mochi*, page 75) and Mochi Dusted with Roasted Green Soybean Flour (*Uguisu Mochi*, page 72).

5. Kanbaiko

Sweet *mochi* rice is steam cooked, then pounded into a rice cake (*mochi*). The *mochi* is then baked, dried, and milled into a very fine powder. Used primarily in making Shiso Mochi Cake (*Shiogama*, page 86) and Traditional Tea Ceremony Sweet (*Higashi*, page 89).

6. Kuzuko

Kuzuko is a starch extracted from the root of the arrowroot plant by pounding the root then soaking the starch extract in water, and then drying the liquid. The starch is hard to extract, so it is rare to find *kuzuko* that is 100% made from arrowroot. Often, it is mixed with potato or corn starch. The arrowroot plant is mainly found in the Nara and Fukuoka prefectures. *Kuzuko* is used to make Japanese Arrowroot Jelly with Red Bean and Salted Cherry Blossom (*Kuzuzakura*, page 78) and Rice Flour and Arrowroot Dessert (*Uiro*, page 80).

7. Warabiko

Warabiko is a starch extracted from the root of the bracken plant, a type of fern. Like *kuzuko*, the extraction process is difficult, and store-bought *warabiko* often contains potato or corn starch. *Warabiko* is used to make Bracken Starch Mochi with Roasted Soybean Flour (*Warabi Mochi*, page 85).

8. Kinako and Uguisu Kinako

Yellow soybeans are roasted and milled to make *kinako*. Used in Roasted Soybean Powder Sweet Mochi Rice Balls (*Ohagi*, page 64), and when combined with sugar, it is used as a coating on grilled *mochi* to impart a roasted aroma. When made with green soybeans, the flour is called *Uguisu Kinako*, and is used to make Mochi Dusted with Roasted Green Soybean Flour (*Uguisu Mochi*, page 72).

Wagashi Tools

1. Japanese Tamises with 5mm Mesh Openings There are three types of Japanese tamises (also called drum sieves). Stainless steel ones (*kinzoku furui*) are durable, easy to maintain and strong enough to mill bean paste as well as strain liquids. Horsehair drum sieves (*umage furui*) are made from woven horsehair. They are flexible and ideal for making smooth pastes. Lastly, there are sieves made from woven bamboo (*kinton burui*). These are favored for making Golden Sweet Bean Paste (*Kinton Nerikeri*, p. 33).

2. Food Processor Essential for quick, even, and efficient mixing.

3. Scale The precise measurement of ingredients is important in making *wagashi*, and you'll find most ingredient amounts listed in grams. Your scale should be able to weigh quantities under 10 grams.

4. Large Pastry Brush for dusting or brushing off excess flour.

5. Wooden Spatula to mix and stir bean paste (*an*). Choose one that is sturdy and feels comfortable in your hand.

6. Rolling Pin to roll out dough.

7. Whisk to mix liquid ingredients.

8. Measuring Cup A plastic measuring cup comes in handy when weighing wet or dry ingredients. Place the cup on a kitchen scale, then hit the tare button to account for the weight of the cup. Add the ingredient to the cup until you reach the weight called for in the recipe.

9. Bowl A large, deep mixing bowl with a stable base is the most useful.

10. Handled Sieve A handled sieve can be placed over a bowl to sift dry ingredients or strain liquids.

11. Mortar and Pestle to grind edamame and other ingredients.

12. Rectangular Stainless Steel Molds Small, medium, and large rectangular molds are used for sweet bean- and jelly-type *wagashi*.

13. Triangular Stainless Steel Molds Long molds for making sweet bean jelly *wagashi* (*yokan*). Other styles in half-moon and square shapes are also available.

14. Higashi Wooden Molds These handcrafted molds are traditionally used for making delicate Japanese tea ceremony sweets (*higashi*). Molds that make multiple, smaller-sized *wagashi* at once are especially convenient.

15. Nerikiri Wooden Molds These are designed specifically for bean paste sweets (*nerikiri*). They are made by professionally trained mold masters, and therefore pricey, but desserts come out of them looking perfect.

16. Deep Stainless Steel Tray This comes in handy for a number of steps, from dusting desserts with flavored powders to shaping *wagashi*.

17. Thin Cooking Chopsticks These are much longer than chopsticks used for eating. Ones with narrow tips are easier to use when working with desserts that have intricate detailing.

18. Small Pastry Brush for adding finishing touches on desserts. A brush with narrow bristles is easier to use.

19. Stainless Steel Cookie Cutters A Japanese maple leaf is one of the traditional *wagashi* shapes, but choose any shape you like.

20. Porcelain Molds Used for agar-agar and arrowroot-based jelly sweets (*kingyoku*, *mizu manju* and others).

21. Cotton Cheesecloth to shape bean paste into balls and for keeping your hands moist when working with bean pastes.

22. Bamboo Mat (*makisu*) The kind of mat used for sushi rolls can also be used to make *wagashi*. The standard size has a width of 11 inches (28 cm). Make sure to wash and thoughly dry the mat after every use.

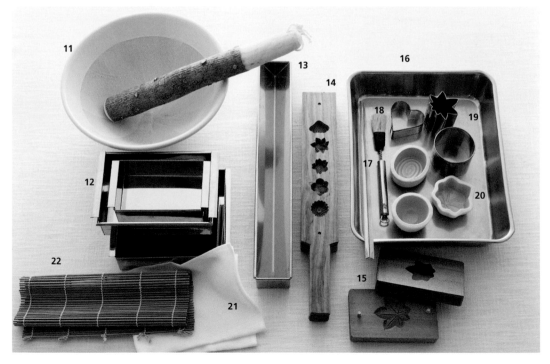

Machiko "MC" Wagashi Molds and Tools

Traditionally, *wagashi* are made using wooden molds that are hand-carved by master craftsmen. I have developed more efficient and affordable plastic molds that are easy to use.

Nerikiri Molds

These molds are for making bean paste sweets (*nerikiri*). Each series contains three shapes, plus a pastry scraper.

Flower series: chrysanthemum (A), plum blossom (B), and cherry blossom (C)

A

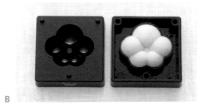

B

C

Leaf series: Japanese maple leaf (A), gourd (B), and autumn leaf (C)

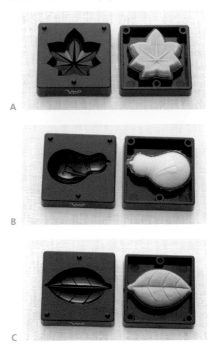

A

B

C

Cat series: beckoning lucky cat (A), cat paw (B), and cat silhouette (C)

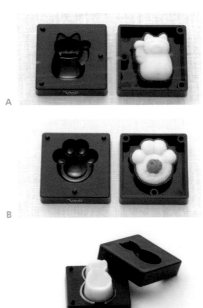

A

B

C

Nerikiri Push Molds

Bean paste sweets can also be made with push molds. Push the bean paste through the tube to make the shape. Each series contains four molds:

Classic Series: large round (A), small round (B), large square (C), and small square (D)

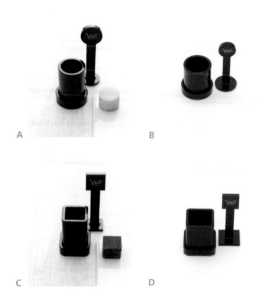

A   B

C   D

Japanese Tamis

A tamis, also called a drum sieve, is used to puree ingredients and to make small strands of bean paste that are used to decorate *wagashi*.

Seasonal Series: cherry blossom (A), gourd (B), Japanese maple leaf (C), and heart (D)

A   B

C   D

Higashi Mold

This mold is for making traditional Japanese tea ceremony sweets. It makes six of them at once.

Nagashikan Mold

This rectangular mold with a removable bottom is used for *yokan*, *kingyoku*, and other jelly-type *wagashi*.

Wagashi Color Palette

Using beautiful colors is an important visual element in making traditional Japanese sweets. Subtle colors are preferred, but it is also fun to experiment with variations.

Sample Colors:

Green and yellow make a pale green (A)
Red and yellow make orange, the color of persimmons (B)
Blue and red make violet (C)
Blue and green make aqua (D)

Fruit and Vegetable Colors:

Adding pureed fruits and vegetables to white bean paste is a great way to impart natural color, flavor, and fragrance. Be sure to take water content into consideration. Start with a fairly firm bean paste so it does not become too soft after adding the puree.

1. Kabocha (Japanese Squash)

Cut and peel 100g of kabocha into small 3cm cubes. Heat in the microwave for 5 minutes with the steam holes of the Cook-Zen set to "close." Press the squash through a tamis.

2. Blueberries

Cook a handful of blueberries in the microwave for 1 minute with the steam holes of the Cook-Zen set to "close." Press the berries through a tamis.

3. Raspberries

Cook a handful of raspberries for 1 minute in the microwave with the steam holes of the Cook-Zen set to "close." Press the berries through a tamis.

4. Edamame

Cook 100g edamame pods in the microwave for 2 minutes with the steam holes of the Cook-Zen set to "close." Shell the edamame, peel off the skins, then grind the beans using a mortar and pestle.

Wagashi Calendar

January The New Year's celebration is seen everywhere throughout Japan. Our families and friends get together to wish each other good health. We go to temples and shrines to pray, to make resolutions and promises to work harder. Red and White Sweet Bean Paste Dessert (*Kohaku Nerikiri*) is popular to give and receive as a gift, as this dessert is said to bring good fortune. Golden Sweet Bean Paste (*Kinton Nerikiri*) and Chestnut and Red Bean Jelly (*Kuri-Yokan*) are favored seasonal gifts as well.

February We long for the warm spring weather to arrive. In Japan, the plum tree (*ume*) flowers start to blossom shyly, a hint of good things to come. The adorable shapes of the blossoms and the sweet fragrance and fresh flavor of the plums inspire sweets such as Japanese Plum Compote (*Ume Amani*) and Green Plum Rice Cakes (*Aoume Daifuku*).

March Spring arrives slowly, bringing hope and rebirth. *Mochi* Dusted with Green Soybean Flour (*Uguisu Mochi*) is a popular seasonal *wagashi*, representing a yellow-green Japanese nightingale that sings joyously in spring. We celebrate "Girl's Day" on the 3rd of March by sharing Cherry Blossom Rice Cakes (*Domyoji Sakura Mochi*).

April Cherry blossoms are now in full bloom. To reflect the season, *wagashi* are made in varying shades of pink and green, and are molded into different spring motifs. Cherry Blossom Sweet Bean Jelly (*Sakura Yokan*) is the perfect accompaniment to afternoon tea.

May This month sees magnificent blue sky and sunny days. To enjoy this month, full of vivid and lively spring colors, Polka Dot Agar-Agar Jelly (*Mizutama Kingyoku*) can be served to guests. Camellia Rice Cakes (*Tsubaki Mochi*) are also a staple, as camellias are in season.

June In June, monsoons bring daily rains and high humidity. Traditionally, we Japanese have found creative ways to find joy despite the inclement weather. As purple-blue hydrangeas bloom, we enjoy bean paste sweets (*nerikiri*) colored with blueberries, which are in season.

July This is the season when we eagerly await the arrival of the summer sun. Toward the end of this month, streams in the mountains become clear and bright. The *wagashi* called Tri-Color Beans in White Curaçao Jelly (*Seiryu*) recreates the water and colorful pebbles.

August A chilled dessert is welcome during this hot and humid month. Sweet Red Bean Jelly (*Mizu Yokan*), made with a perfectly balanced combination of red bean paste and agar-agar, has a refined, soft texture that will melt in your mouth. It is the perfect dessert to make you feel refreshed.

September The temperature cools, welcoming a delightful season full of traditional cultural festivities. Sweet Mochi Rice Balls (*Ohagi*) are one of Japan's most traditional desserts, usually enjoyed during this time of year when *hagi*, a bush clover plant, appears. *Ohagi* is made from coarsely ground rice, steam cooked, then shaped into a ball before being covered in smooth red bean paste.

October We enjoy the transitory nature of the season, highlighted by brilliant displays of foliage wherever we go. We tend to use traditional bowls and plates that are more subdued in color, simpler in design. Chrysanthemums, chestnuts, and other autumnal vegetables and flowers inspire *wagashi* at this time of year. My recipe for Chestnut Parfait (Mont Blanc aux Marrons) captures the spirit of the season.

November Toward the end of the year, the sweet bean pastes (*nerikiri*) served at tea ceremonies represent the vibrant colors of autumn— orange, green, and yellow—in the shapes of different leaves. A classic example is Maple Leaf-Shaped Sweet Bean Paste (*Momiji Nerikiri*).

December This is when we begin our preparations to welcome the New Year. Traditional Tea Ceremony Sweets (*Higashi*) can be made in advance of this busy holiday. They keep well and are perfect for unexpected visits from friends and family.

Sweet Bean Paste Wagashi
(Nerikiri)

Lily Bulbs

If someone were to ask me what is the most important ingredient for making *wagashi*, I would answer sweet bean paste or *an*.

Traditional bean paste is made from either red beans (*azuki*) or white beans (*shiro-azuki* or *shiro-insen*). Today you can find many other flavor variations, including green tea (matcha), sweet potato, pumpkin, blueberry, even chocolate.

The recipes in this chapter use bean powder, which makes the preparation of bean paste very simple compared to the traditional cooking method.

Red and White
Sweet Bean Paste Dessert
(*Kohaku Nerikiri*)

Equipment/Tools:
- Wooden spatula
- 2 bowls
- Plastic wrap

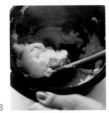

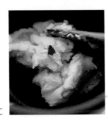

With the Cook-Zen pot and white bean powder, you can make this classic *wagashi* in just 3 minutes.

Makes 10 pieces

White Bean Paste:
100g white bean powder
100g sugar
Pinch of salt
200g water
1 scant drop red food coloring*

1 Set your microwave to a power level of 600 watts (see page 12 for more information).

2 To make the white bean paste, place the white bean powder, sugar, salt, and water in the Cook-Zen and mix well.

3 Cover and heat for 3 minutes with the steam holes set to "close." Carefully open and mix with a wooden spatula until smooth. Let cool.

4 Divide the white bean paste equally into two separate bowls.

5 Carefully add a scant drop of food coloring to one bowl of bean paste. Mix until the paste is evenly colored. If needed, carefully add an additional drop to deepen the color, but remember that a little goes a long way.

6 Equally divide the white bean paste and red bean paste into 10 portions each. Place a portion of white paste next to a portion red paste on a sheet of plastic wrap (about 8 x 11 inches). Gently wrap the plastic around the paste and shape it into a round ball in the palm of your hand, twisting the wrap on top. Then, gently remove the wrap.

* When using powdered coloring, make sure to dissolve the powder in one or two drops of water. Add one drop at a time to color the paste.

Green Tea-Flavored Sweet Bean Paste Dessert

(*Matcha Nerikiri*)

Equipment/Tools:
- Small bowl
- Wooden spatula
- Push mold, any shape

Matcha has become increasingly popular, thanks to the green tea's flavor and antioxidant properties. The flavor of matcha is complex, with a pronounced bitterness that complements the bean paste's subtle hint of sweetness.

Makes 10 pieces

20g water
1 teaspoon matcha powder

White Bean Paste:
100g white bean paste powder
100g sugar
Pinch of salt
180g water
Gold leaf, for garnish (optional)

1 Set your microwave to a power level of 600 watts (see page 12 for more information).

2 In a small bowl, combine 20g water and the matcha powder. Mix well.

3 To make the bean paste, place the white bean paste powder, sugar, salt, 180g water, and the matcha mixture in the Cook-Zen. Mix well. Cover and heat for 3 minutes with the steam holes set to "close." Carefully open the lid and mix with a wooden spatula until the matcha paste is smooth. Let cool.

4 Divide the matcha bean paste into 10 equal portions, rolling each into a ball.

5 Place a matcha paste ball into the push mold and press until all the paste has gone through. The *nerikiri* should be about ¾-inch thick. Garnish each piece with a small fleck of gold leaf before serving.

Lily Bulb Sweet Bean Paste Dessert

(Yuri-ne Nerikiri)

Equipment/Tools:
- Tamis (Japanese-style drum sieve)
- Wooden spatula
- Plastic wrap

A

Lily bulbs (yuri-ne) have a light sweet taste, reminiscent of Japanese sweet potatoes. Here I've added them to bean paste for a delicate, appealing flavor combination.

Makes 10 pieces

1 large (about 130 g) lily bulb

White Bean Paste:
100g white bean powder
100g sugar
Pinch of salt
200g water

Gold leaf, for garnish (optional)

1 Set your microwave to a power level of 600 watts (see page 12 for more information).

2 Wash the lily bulb and remove any dirt or damaged parts with a knife. Pat the bulb dry and place it in the Cook-Zen. Cover and cook for 2 ½ to 3 minutes with the steam holes set to "close."

3 Press the cooked lily bulb through the tamis with a wooden spatula to puree it (A).

4 To make the white bean paste, place the white bean powder, sugar, salt, and water in the Cook-Zen and mix well.

5 Cover and heat (at 600 watts) for 3 minutes with the steam holes set to "close." Carefully open and mix with the wooden spatula until smooth. Let cool.

6 Add the cooked lily bulb to the white bean paste and mix until smooth. Let cool completely, then divide into 10 equal portions.

7 Place a portion of the bean paste mixture on a piece of plastic wrap (about 8 x 11 inches). Gently roll it into a ball in the palm of your hand and twist the plastic wrap on top. Then gently remove the wrap.

8 Garnish each piece with a small fleck of gold leaf.

Golden Sweet Bean Paste

(*Kinton Nerikiri*)

Equipment/Tools:

- Wooden spatula
- Bamboo or plastic tamis with 5mm holes (*kinton burui*, see page 18)
- Tray or plate
- Cooking chopsticks (thin)

A

B

C

This sweet is similar in color to the chestnut and sweet potato paste *wagashi* (*kuri kinton*) served at Japanese New Year's celebrations. The strands that decorate the *wagashi* are made by pressing bean paste through the holes of a bamboo tamis. The key to making a good *kinton* is keeping the bean paste moist.

Makes 10 pieces

White Bean Paste:

Drop of yellow food coloring
240g water
100g white bean powder
100g sugar
Pinch of salt

1 Set your microwave to a power level of 600 watts (see page 12 for more information).

2 To make the white bean paste, add one drop of yellow food coloring to the water and mix. Add it to the Cook-Zen along with the white bean powder, sugar, and salt. Mix well. Cover and heat for 2 ½ to 3 minutes with the steam holes set to "close." Carefully open the lid and mix with the wooden spatula until the mixture comes together. Let cool.

3 To create the strands of bean paste, take ⅔ of the bean paste mixture and place it on the tamis. Press the paste down through the sieve while simultaneously pulling the paste towards you (A). The strands should resemble thin noodles (B).

4 Divide the remaining bean paste into 10 equal pieces and shape into balls. Place the bean paste balls onto a tray and, using chopsticks, decorate each bean paste ball with the strands (C).

Gourd- and Japanese Maple Leaf-Shaped Sweet Bean Paste

(Hyotan and Momiji Nerikiri)

Equipment/Tools:

- Wooden spatula
- 2 bowls
- Wooden or plastic molds (gourd and maple leaf shapes)
- Pastry scraper (see page 20)

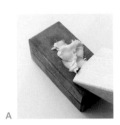

A

B

Makes 8 pieces

White Bean Paste:
100g white bean powder
100g sugar
Pinch of salt
180g water

1 scant drop each of green, red, and yellow food coloring

1 Set your microwave to a power level of 600 watts (see page 12 for more information).

2 To make the white bean paste, place the white bean powder, sugar, salt, and water in the Cook-Zen and mix well.

3 Cover and heat for 3 minutes with the steam holes set to "close." Carefully open and mix with the wooden spatula until smooth. Let cool.

4 Divide the bean paste into two equal portions and place them in bowls. Add the green food coloring to one portion, mixing until it is a uniform color. This green paste is for the gourd-shaped mold. Next, add the red and yellow food coloring to the second portion of bean paste and mix well. The orange color, resembling persimmons, is used for the Japanese maple leaf mold.

5 Quickly rinse gourd mold under cold running water and wipe off any excess moisture with a cloth or paper towel (this helps keep the bean paste from sticking to a wooden mold). Place the green bean paste in the mold, filling it from the top and making sure to press it in firmly. Remove the excess paste from the top of the mold using a spatula or a pastry scraper (A).

6 To unmold the bean paste, open the mold from the middle (B), and carefully turn it upside down. Gently tap a corner of the mold against a hard surface to ease out the sweet.

7 Repeat with remaining bean paste and the maple leaf mold.

Blueberry-Flavored Sweet Bean Paste

(*Blueberry Nerikiri*)

Equipment/Tools:
- Wooden spatula
- Round or square push mold
- Tamis (Japanese-style drum sieve)
- Cooking chopsticks

Tart blueberries lend this dessert an appealing purple hue, and their flavor combines deliciously with the sweet bean paste. Use the round or square push mold for beautiful geometric shapes.

Makes 8 pieces

100g blueberries

White Bean Paste:
70g white bean powder
70g sugar
140g water
Pinch of salt
Silver leaf, for garnish
Purple or silver dragees (edible sugar pearls), for garnish

1 Set your microwave to a power level of 600 watts (see page 12 for more information).

2 Wash and dry the blueberries. Place in the Cook-Zen and heat for 2 minutes with the steam holes set to "close." Press the cooked blueberries through the tamis to puree them. Set aside.

3 Rinse the Cook-Zen. To make the white bean paste, place the white bean powder, sugar, water, and salt in the Cook-Zen and mix well. Cover and heat (at 600 watts) for 2 minutes with the steam holes set to "close." Carefully open and mix with the wooden spatula until smooth. Let cool.

4 Add the blueberry puree to the bean paste, a little at a time, and mix until uniform in color. The paste should have a consistency that is firmer than an earlobe (a Japanese expression that is hard to translate!).

5 Set aside two-thirds of the bean paste for the garnish. Divide the remaining bean paste into 8 equal portions, rolling each into a ball. Place a bean paste ball into the mold and gently push the paste out (A).

6 Place the blueberry paste that you've set aside for the garnish on the tamis. Press the paste down through the sieve while simultaneously pulling towards you to make short strands.

7 Using cooking chopsticks, delicately cover the top of the bean paste shapes with the strands. Garnish with silver leaf and dragees.

Sweet Bean Paste Desserts in Seasonal Motifs

(*Nerikiri*)

Equipment/Tools:

- Wooden spatula
- 3 bowls
- Nerikiri molds (chrysanthemum, cherry blossom, and Japanese maple leaf shapes)
- Pastry scraper

A

B

C

D

Celebrate the seasons of Japan by using flower and leaf designs in different color combinations.

Makes 6 assorted pieces

White Bean Paste:
100g white bean powder
100g sugar
Pinch of salt
180g water
1 scant drop each of green, pink, and yellow food coloring

1 Set your microwave to a power level of 600 watts (see page 12 for more information).

2 To make the white bean paste, place the white bean powder, sugar, salt, and water in the Cook-Zen and mix well.

3 Cover and heat for 3 minutes with the steam holes set to "close." Carefully open and mix with a wooden spatula until smooth. Let cool.

4 Divide the paste among 3 separate bowls.

5 Add a scant drop of green coloring to one bowl, red in another, and yellow in the third. Mix until the color of the bean paste is uniform.

6 Fill a mold with bean paste by hand, pressing until the mold is completely filled to eliminate any trapped air bubbles (B).

7 Level the mold with a spatula or pastry scraper, taking off any excess paste (C).

8 To unmold the bean paste, turn the mold upside down, open it, tap the mold gently, and carefully remove the *nerikiri* (D).

9 Repeat with the remaining bean paste and mold shapes.

* Note: When using the cherry blossom mold, you can create a shape with two layers of petals (*yaezakura*) by gently opening the mold ¼ inch and then twisting the mold a quarter turn in either direction before completely opening the mold to remove the bean paste blossom.

Cat-shaped Sweet Bean Paste Desserts

(*Neko Nerikiri*)

Equipment/Tools:
- Wooden spatula
- 2 bowls
- Sieve
- Whisk
- *Nerikiri* molds (cat series)
- Pastry scraper

A

B

C

D

These shapes are a cat lover's dream.

Makes 10 assorted pieces

White Bean Paste:
100g white bean powder
100g sugar
Pinch of salt
120g water

Agar-Agar:
¼ stick agar-agar (kanten)
100g water

1 Set your microwave to a power level of 600 watts (see page 12 for more information).

2 To make the white bean paste, place the white bean powder, sugar, salt, and 120g water in the Cook-Zen and mix well.

3 Cover and heat for 3 minutes with the steam holes set to "close." Carefully open and mix with a wooden spatula until smooth. Set aside in a bowl and let cool.

4 Tear the agar-agar into very small pieces by hand. Place the pieces in a sieve and quickly rinse under cold water. Squeeze out the excess water. Rinse the Cook-Zen and place the agar-agar inside. Pour in 100g of water, and heat (at 600 watts) for 4 minutes with the steam holes set to "close."

5 Whisk the agar-agar liquid and strain it into a bowl, using the sieve. Pour the strained liquid into the bowl containing the white bean paste and quickly mix until everything is combined (A).

6 Fill a mold with the mixture, making sure to press firmly to eliminate any spaces (B). Remove any excess paste with a scraper.

7 To unmold the *nerikiri*, take off the top half of the mold. Turn the mold over and gently tap one corner to help loosen the sweet, then carefully remove it (D).

* **Variation:** You can make a brown cat by substituting an equal amount of red bean powder for the white bean powder. For added effect, make a cat's tail and collar with any extra bean paste.

Bean Paste with Egg Yolk
(*Kimishigure*)

Equipment/Tools:
- Wooden spatula
- Tamis (Japanese-style drum sieve)
- Bowl

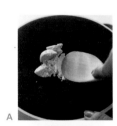

This is one of the most popular sweets served at Japanese tea ceremonies.

Note: Make sure to set the steam holes to "close" in step 3, and then "open" in step 7.

Makes 10 pieces

White Bean Paste:
100g white bean powder
100g sugar
Pinch of salt
200g water

3 warm, hard-boiled egg yolks
3 tablespoons heavy cream
15 to 30g sugar
1 raw egg yolk

1 Set your microwave to a power level of 600 watts (see page 12 for more information).

2 To make the white bean paste, place the white bean powder, 100g sugar, salt, and water in the Cook-Zen and mix well.

3 Close the lid and heat the mixture for 2 ½ minutes with the steam holes set to "close." Carefully open the lid and mix until combined.

4 While the hard-boiled egg yolks are still warm, use the wooden spatula to press them through the tamis and into a bowl (A).

5 Mix the mashed egg yolk with the white bean paste. Add heavy cream, 15 to 30g sugar, and the raw egg yolk and mix well (B).

6 Divide the mixture into 10 equal pieces and form them into balls. Each should weigh about 30g.

7 Rinse the Cook-Zen and place 5 of the bean paste balls inside. Cover and heat (at 600 watts) for about 1 ½ minutes with the steam holes set to "open." Wait until the pieces are completely cooled to the touch before taking them out, since they may crumble when warm. Repeat with the remaining pieces.

Sweet Red Bean Jelly

(*Mizu Yokan*)

Equipment/Tools:
- Wooden spatula
- 2 bowls
- Sieve
- Whisk
- 2 large bowls
- 14 x 11 x 4.5cm rectangular mold

Red bean jelly (*yokan*) is a cool, refreshing example of traditional Japanese *wagashi*.

Makes one bar of *yokan*

Red Bean Paste:
70g red bean powder
70g sugar
140g water

Agar-Agar:
1/3 stick agar-agar (kanten)
300g water

15 to 30g sugar
1/3 teaspoon salt

1 Set your microwave to a power level of 600 watts (see page 12 for more information).

2 To make the red bean paste, mix together red bean powder, sugar, and 140g of water in the Cook-Zen.

3 Close the lid and heat for 2 minutes with the steam holes set to "close." After cooking, mix with a wooden spatula until the paste is combined, then set aside in a bowl.

4 To make the sweet red bean jelly, shred the agar-agar into small pieces by hand and place in a sieve (A). Rinse under cold water, then squeeze the agar-agar to remove any excess water.

5 Rinse the Cook-Zen, then add 300g of water and the shredded agar-agar. Close the lid and heat (at 600 watts) for 5 minutes with the steam holes set to "close."

6 Whisk the agar-agar liquid and strain it into a bowl, using the sieve (B). Add the agar-agar liquid, sugar, and salt to the red bean paste and mix until smooth.

7 Pour the mixture into the mold (C), and chill in the refrigerator until set (D), about 20 to 30 minutes. Slice or cut into shapes before serving.

Ginger and Red Bean Jelly
(*Shoga Yokan*)

Tools:

- Sieve
- Whisk
- 2 bowls
- 14 x 11 x 4.5cm rectangular mold

A

You'll be pleasantly surprised by this flavor combination. The touch of heat from the julienned ginger complements the sweetness of the jelly. Enjoy!

Makes one bar of *yokan*

Candied Ginger:
50g fresh ginger
80g water
60g sugar

Red Bean Paste:
100g red bean powder
100g sugar
200g water

Agar-Agar:
1 stick agar-agar (kanten)
150g water

30g sugar
1/8 teaspoon salt

1 Set your microwave to a power level of 600 watts (see page 12 for more information).

2 To make the candied ginger, julienne the ginger and place it in the Cook-Zen. Add 80g of water, close the lid, and heat for 3 minutes with the steam holes set to "close" (A).

3 Add 60g sugar to the cooked ginger. Close the lid and heat (at 600 watts) for 8 additional minutes with the steam holes set to "close." After cooking, set the ginger aside in a bowl to cool. Rinse the Cook-Zen.

4 To make the red bean paste, mix together the red bean powder, 100g sugar, and 200g of water in the Cook-Zen. Close the lid and heat (at 600 watts) for 3 minutes with the steam holes set to "close." After cooking, mix the paste until it is combined and set aside.

5 To make the agar-agar, first shred the agar-agar into small pieces by hand and place in a sieve. Rinse under cold water, then squeeze the agar-agar to remove any excess water.

6 Rinse the Cook-Zen and place the agar-agar inside. Add 150g of water, close the lid, and heat (at 600 watts) for 5 minutes with the steam holes set to "close."

6 After cooking, whisk the agar-agar liquid and strain it into a bowl, using the sieve. Place the liquid back into the Cook-Zen along with the red bean paste, 30g sugar, and salt. Cover and heat (at 600 watts) for 3 to 4 minutes with the steam holes set to "close."

8 Add the cooled ginger to the bean paste mixture and mix until combined. Pour into the mold and chill for 20 to 30 minutes. Slice or cut into shapes before serving.

Chocolate and Red Bean Jelly
(*Chocolate Yokan*)

Equipment/Tools:

• 2 bowls
• Sieve
• Whisk
• 14 x 11 x 4.5cm
  rectangular mold

Chocolate and red bean paste may sound like an unusual flavor combination, but you'll be surprised! This is a wonderful dessert for any occasion.

Makes one bar of yokan

Red Bean Paste:
70g red bean powder
70g sugar
140g water

Agar-Agar:
²/₃ stick agar-agar (kanten)
180g water

1 tablespoon potato starch syrup (mizuame)
50g dark chocolate chips
100g heavy cream

1 Set your microwave to a power level of 600 watts (see page 12 for more information).

2 To make the red bean paste, mix together the red bean powder, sugar, and 140g of water in the Cook-Zen.

3 Close the lid and heat for 2 minutes with the steam holes set to "close."

4 After cooking, mix until the paste is combined, and set aside in a bowl.

5 Rinse the Cook-Zen. Tear the agar-agar by hand over a sieve into small pieces. Rinse under cold water, then squeeze out the excess water and place it in the Cook-Zen. Add 180g water, close the lid and heat (at 600 watts) for 5 minutes with the steam holes set to "close." After cooking, use a sieve to strain the agar-agar liquid into a bowl and set aside.

6 Add the red bean paste and potato starch syrup to the agar-agar mixture and whisk until combined.

7 Rinse the Cook-Zen, then add the chocolate chips along with the heavy cream. Cover and heat (at 600 watts) for 50 seconds with the steam holes set to "close." Whisk until smooth.

8 Add the melted chocolate to the mixture from step 6. Whisk to combine, pour into the mold, and let it cool in the refrigerator for 20 to 30 minutes until set.

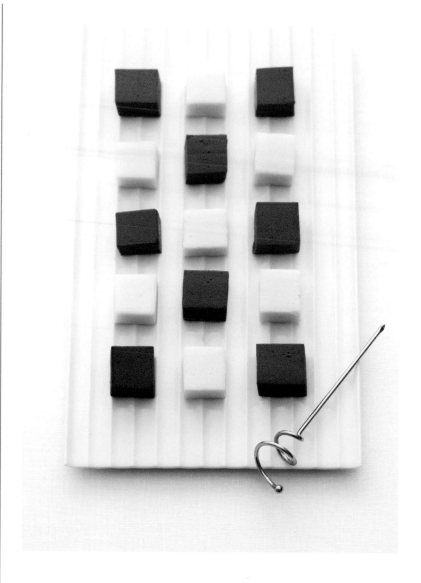

* **Variation:** You can also make a white chocolate version of this *yokan* recipe. Simply substitute an equal amount of white chocolate chips for the regular chocolate and the same amount of white bean powder for the red bean powder.

Candied-Bean Jelly *(Amanatto Yokan)*

3 Variations:
Fresh Spring Green-Pea Jelly (*Uguisu Yokan*)
Cherry Blossom Sweet Bean Jelly (*Sakura Yokan*)
Dark Sweet Bean Jelly (*Kuro Amanatto Yokan*)

Equipment/Tools:
- Sieve
- Whisk
- Large bowl
- Food processor
- Rubber spatula
- 2 round ice cube trays (for Fresh Spring Green-Pea Jelly and Dark Sweet Bean Jelly) or 1 17 x 14 x 4.5 cm rectangular mold and cookie cutters (for Cherry Blossom Sweet Bean Jelly)

A

Candied beans are a traditional Japanese sweet made by boiling beans in a mixture of sugar and water. They are usually sold in plastic pouches and several varieties are available, from green peas to white kidney beans, giving you the ability to transform plain *yokan* into colorful desserts. To achieve a smooth texture, try to select candied beans that are soft so that they puree more thoroughly.

Makes 20 to 28 pieces

1 stick agar-agar (kanten)
200g water
250g candied green peas (uguisu mame)
60g sugar

To Make the Agar-Agar (*Kanten*) for All Three Variations:

1 Set your microwave to a power level of 600 watts (see page 12 for more information).

2 Tear the agar-agar into small pieces by hand over a sieve. Rinse under cold water and squeeze out the excess water by hand.

3 Place the agar-agar and 200g of water in the Cook-Zen. Close the lid and heat (at 600 watts) for 4 to 5 minutes with the steam holes set to "close." After cooking, whisk to combine and strain the liquid into a bowl.

Fresh Spring Green-Pea Jelly
(*Uguisu Yokan*)

4 Add the candied green peas to the food processor and lightly puree. Then add the agar-agar liquid (from step 3), along with the sugar and puree until smooth and thick, using a rubber spatula to check the consistency. Divide the mixture among two round ice cube trays (A) and chill in the refrigerator until firm. When set, unmold the jellies.

Cherry Blossom Sweet Bean Jelly
(Sakura Yokan)

Makes enough for a 17 x 14 x 4.5cm mold

1 stick agar-agar (kanten)
200g water
1 scant drop red food coloring
250g candied white kidney beans (shiro amanatto)
60g sugar

4 Add a scant drop of the red food coloring to the agar-agar liquid
(from step 3) and then combine with the candied white beans and
sugar in a food processor. Puree until smooth. Pour the mixture into
a 17 x 14 x 4.5cm rectangular mold and chill in the refrigerator until firm.
When set, remove from the mold and use cookie cutters to
cut out desired shapes.

Dark Sweet Bean Jelly
(Kuro Amanatto Yokan)

Makes 20 to 28 pieces

1 stick agar-agar (kanten)
200g water
250g candied red kidney beans (kuro amanatto)
60g sugar

4 Place the candied red beans in a food processor. Add the agar-agar
liquid (from step 3) and the sugar. Puree until smooth. Divide the mixture
among two round ice cube trays and chill in the refrigerator until firm.
When set, unmold the jellies.

Lily Bulb in Sweet White Bean Jelly

(*Yuri-ne Yokan*)

Equipment/Tools:
- Tamis (Japanese-style drum sieve)
- Wooden spatula
- Sieve
- Whisk
- 3 bowls
- 3 x 30 cm triangular mold or 14 x 11 x 4.5 cm rectangular mold

Lily bulb and white bean paste make for an elegant white-on-white combination. If you like, add coloring for a more festive dessert.

Makes 1 bar of *yokan*

Lily Bulb and White Bean Paste:
1 large fresh lily bulb (about 130g)
70g white bean powder
70g sugar
140g water

Agar-Agar:
½ stick agar-agar (kanten)
200g water
Pinch of salt

1 Set your microwave to a power level of 600 watts (see page 12 for more information).

2 Wash the lily bulb and remove any dirt or damaged parts with a knife. Pat dry and place the bulb in the Cook-Zen. Cover and cook for 2 ½ to 3 minutes with the steam holes set to "close."

3 Press the cooked lily bulb through the tamis with a wooden spatula to puree it. Set aside in a bowl.

4 Rinse the Cook-Zen, then place the white bean powder, sugar, and 140g water inside. Mix well. Cover and heat (at 600 watts) for 2 minutes with the steam holes set to "close." Carefully open and mix with the wooden spatula until smooth. Add the pureed lily bulb to the bean paste, mix well, and set aside in a bowl to cool.

5 Tear the agar-agar into small pieces by hand over a sieve. Rinse under cold water and squeeze out any excess water by hand.

6 Rinse the Cook-Zen and place the agar-agar inside with 200g of water. Close the lid, set the steam holes to "close" and heat (at 600 watts) for 5 minutes. After cooking, whisk and strain the liquid into a bowl.

7 Add salt and the lily bulb paste to the agar-agar liquid and mix until combined. Pour into the triangular mold and let set in the refrigerator for 20 to 30 minutes. When set, slice into triangles. If using the rectangular mold, cut the *yokan* in half lengthwise, then cut the yokan crosswise twice, for a total of 6 rectangles. Then, cut each rectangle on the diagonal to make triangles.

Sweet Bean Soups (*Oshiruko*)

3 Variations:
Traditional Sweet Red Bean Soup with Rice Cakes (*Oshiruko*)
Sweet White Bean Soup with Rice Dumplings (*Shiroan Oshiruko*)
Sweet Green Tea Soup with Rice Dumplings (*Matcha Oshiruko*)

Sweet bean soup is a classic Japanese dessert, traditionally made with red beans (*azuki*). One day, a craving for sweet white bean soup inspired me to create some new flavor combinations. Here are two unexpected variations that are sure to please the most sophisticated palate. For those who like the traditional recipe, I've included that, too.

- Wooden spatula
- Small ladle
- 4 serving bowls

Traditional Sweet Red Bean Soup with Rice Cakes (*Oshiruko*)

Makes 4 servings

Red Bean Paste:
100g red bean powder
100g sugar
200g water

200g water
Pinch of salt
30 to 45g sugar
2 (100g) rice cakes (mochi)

1 Set your microwave to a power level of 600 watts (see page 12 for more information).

2 To make the red bean paste, mix together the red bean powder, sugar, and 200g water in the Cook-Zen.

3 Close the lid and heat for 3 minutes with the steam holes set to "close." After cooking, mix with a wooden spatula until the paste is combined.

4 To make the soup, add 200g water, salt, and sugar to the red bean paste in the same Cook-Zen. Close the lid and heat (at 600 watts) for 2 ½ to 3 minutes with the steam holes set to "close." Mix well and ladle the mixture into 4 heat-proof decorative bowls.

5 Rinse the Cook-Zen. Cut each rice cake in half and place all four pieces in the Cook-Zen. Close the lid and heat (at 600 watts) for 30 to 40 seconds with the steam holes set to "close."

6 Place a rice cake into each bowl and serve immediately. Enjoy.

Equipment/Tools:
- 2 bowls
- Wooden spatula
- Small ladle
- 4 serving bowls

Sweet White Bean Soup with Rice Dumplings (*Shiroan Oshiruko*)

Rice dumplings have a texture that is softer and less chewy than *mochi*.

Makes 4 servings

Rice Dumplings:
100g shiratamako rice flour (see page 16)
90g plus 90g water

White Bean Paste:
100g white bean powder
100g sugar
200g water

150g water
Pinch of salt
30 to 45g sugar

Gold leaf, for garnish

1 To make the rice dumplings, combine the rice flour and 90g of water in a bowl and knead until the dough has the firmness of an earlobe (This is a common Japanese expression!).

2 With a teaspoon, place a scoop of dough in the palm of your hand and roll into a ball. Make an indentation in the middle of the ball similar to a thumb-print cookie. (Flattening the center allows for more even heat distribution and cooking of the dough.) Repeat until you have 12 pieces.

3 Set your microwave to a power level of 600 watts (see page 12 for more information).

4 Place 90g of water in the Cook-Zen. Cover and heat for 3 minutes with the steam holes set to "close." Carefully open the lid and place the rice-flour balls in the hot water. Cover and heat (at 600 watts) for 4 more minutes with the steam holes set to "close." When the dough is cooked through, the dumplings will float to the surface. Drain and set aside in a bowl.

5 To make the white bean paste, place the white bean powder, sugar, and 200g water in the Cook-Zen and mix well. Cover and heat (at 600 watts) for 3 minutes with the steam holes set to "close." Carefully open and mix with a wooden spatula. Let cool.

6 To make the soup, add 150g water, salt, and 30 to 45g sugar to the white bean paste in the same Cook-Zen, and mix to combine. Cover and heat (at 600 watts) for 2 ½ to 3 minutes with the steam holes set to "close." Mix well. Add more hot water to lighten the texture, if desired.

7 Ladle the white bean soup into individual serving bowls with one or two rice dumplings in the center. Garnish with a small piece of gold leaf on top before serving.

Equipment/Tools:
- 2 bowls
- Wooden spatula
- Small whisk (used for making salad dressings)
- Small ladle
- 4 serving bowls

Sweet Green Tea Soup with Rice Dumplings (*Matcha Oshiruko*)

Makes 4 servings

Green Tea:
15g green tea powder (matcha)
40g hot water

Rice Dumplings:
100g shiratamako rice flour (see page 16)
90g plus 90g water

White Bean Paste:
100g white bean powder
100g sugar
200g water

30 to 45g sugar
150g water
Pinch of salt

1 In a small bowl, whisk the green tea powder and 40g of hot water until the tea has completely dissolved.

2 To make the rice dumplings, combine the rice flour and 90g of water in a bowl. Mix well until the dough is smooth and has the firmness of an earlobe.

3 Take a teaspoon of dough and roll it into a ball by hand. Make a thumb indentation in the center (for better heat distribution and even cooking). Repeat until you have 12 pieces.

4 Set your microwave to a power level of 600 watts (see page 12 for more information).

5 Add the remaining 90g of water to the Cook-Zen. Close the lid and heat for 3 minutes with the steam holes set to "close." Open carefully and place the shaped dough pieces in the Cook-Zen into the hot water. Close and heat (at 600 watts) for an additional 4 minutes with the steam holes set to "close." Drain and set aside in a bowl.

6 To make the white bean paste, place the white bean powder, 100g of sugar, and 200g of water in the Cook-Zen and mix well.

7 Cover and heat (at 600 watts) for 3 minutes with the steam holes set to "close." Carefully open and mix with the wooden spatula until smooth. Let cool.

8 To make the soup, add 30 to 45g of sugar, 150g of water, salt, and the green tea (from step 1) to the white bean paste in the same Cook-Zen. Mix well with a wooden spatula. Close the lid and heat (at 600 watts) for 2 ½ to 3 minutes with the steam holes set to "close." Mix well. Add more hot water to lighten the texture, if desired.

9 Ladle the sweet bean soup into individual serving bowls. Place two rice dumplings in the middle of each bowl before serving.

Wagashi Made from Rice Flour and
Other Plant-Based Starches

Edamame

Many varieties of rice flour and other plant-based starches are used in traditional Japanese sweets. Most often you'll find *wagashi* made from glutinous rice (*mochi gome*), short-grain Japanese rice (*uruchi mai*), the starch from bracken ferns (*warabi*) and Japanese arrowroot (*kuzu*).

With the Cook-Zen, making these traditional sweets is quick and easy. In this chapter, there are a selection of simple recipes.

Cherry Blossom Rice Cakes

(Domyoji Sakura Mochi)

Equipment/Tools:

• Wooden spatula
• Bowl
• Sieve

A

B

C

This is a staple sweet in spring, when cherry blossoms herald the arrival of the season.

Note: Make sure to set the steam holes to "close" in step 3, and then "open" in step 5. Add just a small amount of food coloring to the rice cake to create the light pink cherry-blossom color. The food coloring darkens when heated—a little goes a long way! It is also important to wrap the red bean paste with the rice while the rice is still warm.

Makes 8 pieces

Red Bean Paste:
60g red bean powder
60g sugar
120g water

Rice:
200g domyojiko rice (see page 16)
200g water
1 scant drop red food coloring
30g sugar
Pinch of salt

8 salted cherry blossom leaves
8 salted cherry blossom flowers

1 Set your microwave to a power level of 600 watts (see page 12 for more information).

2 To make the red bean paste, mix together the red bean powder, 60g of sugar, and 120g of water in the Cook-Zen.

3 Close the lid and heat for 2 minutes with the steam holes set to "close." Mix with a wooden spatula until the paste is combined. Set aside in a separate bowl.

4 Rinse the Cook-Zen and place the rice inside. Give it a quick rinse, then drain the rice using a sieve.

5 Put the drained rice back into the Cook Zen. Add 200g of water, food coloring, 30g of sugar, and salt and mix well (A). Cover and heat (at 600 watts) for 6 to 7 minutes with the steam holes set to "open." After cooking, let it sit for an additional 3 to 4 minutes with the lid on.

6 Divide the red bean paste into 8 equal portions and roll each into a ball.

7 Mix the cooked rice with a wooden spatula (B) and divide into 8 equal portions.

8 While still warm, take a portion of rice and gently flatten it in the palm of your hand. Place one bean-paste ball in the center of the rice and gently fold the rice around it to cover (C). Repeat with remaining rice and red bean paste. Wrap one salted leaf around each rice cake. Lightly rinse the salted cherry blossom flowers, shake dry, and place one on top of each serving.

Camellia Rice Cakes
(*Tsubaki Mochi*)

Equipment/Tools:
- Bowl
- Wooden spatula
- Sieve

This traditional Japanese treat is mentioned in the classic *Tale of Genji*. Enjoy it with a cup of flavorful matcha tea.

Note: Make sure to set the steam holes to "close" in step 3, and then "open" in step 6.

Makes 8 pieces

Red Bean Paste:
60g red bean powder
60g sugar
120g water

Rice:
200g domyojiko rice (see page 16)
200g water
30g sugar
Pinch of salt

16 camellia leaves (tsubaki leaves)

1 Set your microwave to a power level of 600 watts (see page 12 for more information).

2 To make the red bean paste, mix together the red bean powder, 60g of sugar, and 120g of water in the Cook-Zen.

3 Close the lid and heat for 2 minutes with the steam holes set to "close." Then, mix with a wooden spatula until the paste is combined and set aside in a separate bowl.

4 Rinse the Cook-Zen and place the rice inside. Give it a quick rinse, then drain the rice using a sieve.

5 Put the drained rice back into the Cook-Zen. Add 200g of water, 30g of sugar, and salt and mix well.

6 Cover and heat (at 600 watts) for 6 to 7 minutes with the steam holes set to "open." After cooking, let it sit for an additional 3 to 4 minutes with the lid on.

7 Divide the red bean paste into 8 equal portions and roll each into a ball.

8 Mix the cooked rice well with a wooden spatula. Divide into 8 equal portions.

9 While still warm, take one portion of rice and gently flatten it in the palm of your hand. Place one red bean paste ball in the center of the rice and gently fold the rice around it to cover. Repeat with the remaining rice and red bean paste. Sandwich each rice cake between two tsubaki leaves before serving. Do not eat the leaf—it's just decoration!

Sweet Mochi Rice Balls *(Ohagi)*

3 Variations:

Red Bean *(Azuki-an)*

Roasted Soy Bean Powder *(Kinako)*

Black Sesame *(Kurogoma)*

Equipment/Tools:
- Sieve
- 2 shallow bowls
- Food processor
- Large spoon
- Damp cheesecloth

A

B

C

In Japan, everyone grows up eating *ohagi*, so it is considered a "comfort food" by many. Traditionally, it can take a long time to prepare, but with the Cook-Zen and a food processor at hand, this classic treat is very simple to make.

Note: Make sure to set the steam holes to "close" in step 3, and then "open" in step 6.

Makes 12 pieces

Red Bean Paste:
60g red bean powder
60g sugar
120g water

Rice:
400g sweet mochi rice (also called glutinous rice or mochigome)
200g plus 400g water
1/3 teaspoon salt

Roasted Soy Bean Powder Coating:
45g roasted soy bean powder (kinako)
1/2 tablespoon sugar
Pinch of salt

Black Sesame Coating:
75g ground black sesame (kurogoma)
15g sugar
Pinch of salt

1 Set your microwave to a power level of 600 watts (see page 12 for more information).

2 To make the red bean paste, mix together the red bean powder, 60g of sugar, and 120g of water in the Cook-Zen.

3 Close the lid and heat for 2 minutes with the steam holes set to "close." Then, mix until the paste is combined and set aside in a separate bowl. Rinse the Cook-Zen.

4 Place the sweet *mochi* rice inside a sieve. Wash the rice by shaking the sieve under running water. Rinse until the water runs clear. Drain well, and place the rice into the Cook-Zen. Add 200g of water and let sit for 30 minutes.

5 Drain the rice using a sieve and shake off any excess water. Place in a food processor and pulse a few times (A) until the rice grains are halved, but not too finely cut.

6 Place the broken rice back into the Cook-Zen and add 400g of water and ⅓ teaspoon of salt. Cover and heat (at 600 watts) for 13 minutes with the steam holes set to "open." After cooking, let it sit, covered, for 3 minutes, then open and mix with a rice paddle or a large spoon (B).

7 Place the *kinako* and black sesame into two separate shallow bowls. To the *kinako*, add ½ tablespoon of sugar and a pinch of salt, and mix well. To the black sesame, add 15g of sugar and a pinch of salt, and mix well.

8 When the rice has cooled a bit, divide it into 3 equal portions. Then divide and roll each portion into 4 balls, for a total of 12. Coat 4 of the rice balls with the *kinako* mixture by rolling it around in the dish. Coat another set of 4 rice balls with the black sesame mixture. To coat the remaining rice balls with red bean paste, first divide the red bean paste into 4 portions. Flatten each portion in the palm of your hand, then place a rice ball in the center and fold the paste around it to cover. Wrap it with a damp cheesecloth to smooth the outer surface (C).

Skewered Rice Cakes
(*Mitarashi Dango*)

Equipment/Tools:

- Whisk
- Bowl
- Wooden spatula
- Cutting board
- Damp cheesecloth
- Bamboo skewers (6 sticks, 15 cm long)
- Pastry brush

Like sweet *mochi* rice balls, rice cakes on a stick are a popular festive food item in Japan. Whether I'm enjoying the cherry blossoms in spring or celebrating the harvest moon in autumn, I'm inspired to make this recipe.

Makes 6 sticks (3 rice cakes per stick)

Sauce:

4 tablespoons soy sauce

75g sugar

2 tablespoons water

10g potato starch

Rice cakes:

100g jyoshinko rice flour (see page 16)

20g mochiko rice flour (see page 16)

20g sugar

200g water

1 Set your microwave to a power level of 600 watts (see page 12).

2 To make the sauce, use a whisk to combine the soy sauce, 75g of sugar, 2 tablespoons of water, and potato starch in the Cook-Zen. Close the lid and heat for 1 to 1 minute and 20 seconds with the steam holes set to "close." After cooking, whisk again to combine and set aside in a separate bowl (A). Rinse the Cook-Zen.

3 To make the rice cakes, place the two types of rice flour, 20g sugar, and 200g water in the Cook-Zen, then mix well using a whisk. Cover and heat (at 600 watts) for 2 ½ minutes with the steam holes set to "close."

4 Carefully uncover and quickly mix the rice mixture with a wooden spatula to make the dough (B).

5 Cover a cutting board with a damp cheesecloth. Roll out the rice dough like a log using the damp cloth (C). Tear off pieces of dough from the log, each weighing about 15g. You should have about 18 pieces.

6 Moisten your hands and roll the rice dough into balls. Place a ball in the damp cheesecloth and lightly flatten it.

7 Moisten a bamboo skewer, then skewer three rounds of dough. Brush a generous amount of sauce on top using a pastry brush, and repeat with the remaining rice cakes.

Big Fortune Rice Cakes
(*Daifuku Mochi*)

Equipment/Tools:
- Wooden spatula
- 2 trays
- Whisk
- Pastry brush

In recent years, I've seen *daifuku mochi* in New York City shops. At first I was surprised to see New Yorkers eating *daifuku*, but now I think it's wonderful to see traditional Japanese *wagashi* being enjoyed internationally.

Makes 3 to 4 pieces

Red Bean Paste:
100g red bean powder
100g sugar
200g water

Dough:
40g shiratamako rice flour (see page 16)
20g mochiko rice flour (see page 16)
100g water
20g sugar

Potato starch, for dusting

1 Set your microwave to a power level of 600 watts (see page 12 for more information).

2 To make the bean paste, place the red bean powder, 100g of sugar, and 200g of water inside the Cook-Zen. Mix well until combined. Close the lid and heat for 3 minutes with the steam holes set to "close." After cooking, mix with a wooden spatula and place the bean paste onto a tray to cool. When cool to the touch, divide into 3 or 4 balls, depending on how large you want the *daifuku* to be.

3 Rinse the Cook-Zen. To make the dough, combine the two types of rice flour, 100g of water, and 20g of sugar in the Cook-Zen. Whisk until all are combined and the mixture is lump-free. Close the lid and heat (at 600 watts) for 3 minutes with the steam holes set to "close." After cooking, mix with a wooden spatula until the dough becomes thick and sticky.

4 Dust the second tray with the potato starch and place the dough on the tray. Dust your hands with the starch and divide the dough into 3 or 4 balls.

5 Dust your hands again with the potato starch and stretch out a ball of dough in the palm of your hand. Place one ball of red bean paste in the center, then wrap the dough around the bean paste and pinch to close the ends. Use a pastry brush to remove any excess potato starch from the wagashi. Repeat with the remaining dough and bean paste. Place closed-side down to serve.

Green Plum Rice Cakes

(*Aoume Daifuku*)

Equipment/Tools:
- Wooden spatula
- 2 trays
- Whisk
- Pastry brush

With this variation on *daifuku*, I wanted to capture the flavor of the Japanese green plums that appear for only a short period in early summer. They add a nice, refreshing flavor to the rice cakes.

Makes 3 to 4 pieces

Red Bean Paste:
100g red bean powder
100g sugar
200g water

Dough:
Green food coloring, one scant drop or less
100g water
40g shiratamako rice flour (see page 16)
20g mochiko rice flour (see page 16)
20g sugar

Potato starch, for dusting
1 or 2 sweet stewed plums (see Note)

Note: To make sweet stewed plums, follow the recipe for Japanese Plum Compote on page 116. You can also use storebought plums that have been preserved in wine. Look for a bottle of plum wine (*umeshu*) with fruit in it.

1 Set your microwave to a power level of 600 watts (see page 12 for more information).

2 To make the bean paste, place the red bean powder, 100g of sugar, and 200g of water inside the Cook-Zen. Mix well until combined. Close the lid and heat for 3 minutes with the steam holes set to "close." After cooking, mix with a wooden spatula and place the bean paste onto a tray to cool. When cool to the touch, divide into 3 or 4 balls, depending on how large you want the daifuku to be.

3 Rinse the Cook-Zen. To make the dough, combine the food coloring with 100g of water. Place the colored water in the Cook-Zen along with the two types of rice flour and 20g of sugar. Whisk until smooth. Close the lid and heat (at 600 watts) for 3 minutes with the steam holes set to "close." Mix with a wooden spatula until the dough thickens.

4 Dust the second tray with the potato starch and place the dough on the tray to cool. Dust your hands with the starch and divide the dough equally into 3 or 4 pieces.

5 Remove the pits from the stewed plums, then finely chop the flesh and set aside.

6 Dust your hands again with the potato starch. Stretch out the dough in the palm of one hand and in the middle of the dough, place a generous pinch of chopped plum followed by one bean paste ball. Wrap the dough around the bean paste and pinch to close the ends.

7 Use the edge of a spoon to make a groove half-way up the *daifuku* to make it look like a Japanese green plum. Remove any excess potato starch from the *wagashi* using a pastry brush. Repeat with the remaining dough and bean paste.

Mochi Dusted with Roasted Green Soybean Flour

(*Uguisu Mochi*)

Equipment/Tools:
- Wooden spatula
- 2 trays
- Sieve
- Tea strainer

A

B

C

This *wagashi* represents spring. Its green color is reminiscent of new leaves. The word *uguisu* refers to a beautiful nightingale which, for the Japanese, signifies the arrival of the season. Making the dough is easy with the Cook-Zen. Keep in mind that the most important step is to mix the dough until it reaches a smooth, thick consistency.

Makes 10 pieces

Red Bean Paste:
30g red bean powder
30g sugar
55g water

Dough:
100g shiratamako rice flour (see page 16)
100g water
15g sugar

Potato starch, for dusting
100g roasted green soybean powder (uguisu kinako)

1 Set your microwave to a power level of 600 watts (see page 12 for more information).

2 To make the bean paste, place the red bean powder, 30g of sugar, and 55g of water inside the Cook-Zen. Mix well, until combined. Close the lid and heat for 1 minute with the steam holes set to "close." After cooking, mix with a wooden spatula and place the bean paste onto a tray to cool.

3 Rinse the Cook-Zen. To make the dough, place the rice flour in the Cook-Zen and gradually add 100g of water to make a paste, mixing it with your hands until the dough has the firmness of an earlobe (A). Form the dough into one ball and place it in the middle of the Cook-Zen.

4 Close the lid and heat (at 600 watts) for 2 to 2 ½ minutes with the steam holes set to "close."

5 After cooking, mix the dough with a wooden spatula until it becomes thick and opaque (B). At this point, add the 15g of sugar one half at a time. Mix until the dough no longer sticks to the spatula. Dust your hands with potato starch and shape the dough into a single large ball, and set aside.

6 On a separate tray, sift the roasted green soybean powder using a sieve, then set aside. Next, divide the red bean paste into 10 balls and set aside.

7 Dust your hands with more potato starch. Divide the dough into 10 pieces. Stretch out a piece of dough into a 3-inch long oval, then place one bean paste ball in the center. Wrap the dough around it and pinch the ends closed. Repeat with the remaining bean paste and dough.

8 Toss the *mochi* in the roasted green soybean powder. Arrange the mochi on a plate, then dust with additional powder on top using a tea strainer or a very fine sieve, if desired (C).

Edamame Rice Cakes
(*Zunda Mochi*)

Equipment/Tools:

- Bowl
- Japanese mortar and pestle
- Rubber spatula

Edamame is a summer staple in Japan. This *wagashi* is the perfect accompaniment to a cold beer on a hot day.

Makes 12 pieces

Rice Dumplings:
100g shiratamako rice flour (see page 16)
90g plus 90g water

Edamame Paste:
500g whole edamame (fresh or frozen)
15g sugar
Pinch of salt

1 Set your microwave to a power level of 600 watts (see page 12).

2 To make the rice dumplings, combine the rice flour and 90g of water in a bowl. Mix well, using your hands, until the dough is smooth and has the firmness of an earlobe.

3 Divide the dough into 12 pieces and roll each into a ball by hand. Make a thumb indentation in the middle to allow for even heat distribution and cooking.

4 Add the remaining 90g of water to the Cook-Zen. Close the lid and heat for 3 minutes with the steam holes set to "close." Open and place the shaped dough pieces in the Cook-Zen with the hot water. Close the lid and heat (at 600 watts) for 4 additional minutes with the steam holes set to "close." When the dumplings are cooked and ready, they should float to the top of the hot water. Drain and set aside.

5 If using fresh edamame to make the paste, rinse them and remove the stems, leaving the pods intact. Place in the Cook-Zen, close the lid, and heat (at 600 watts) for 5 minutes with the steam holes set to "close." If using frozen edamame, heat for 3 to 4 minutes.

6 After the edamame have cooled, take the beans out of the pods and remove the thin skin covering each bean.

7 Place the beans in the mortar and, using the pestle, grind until you get a rough paste (A). At this point, add the sugar and salt and continue to grind until you get a textured paste that still retains some edamame bits (B).

8 Add the rice dumplings to the edamame paste and gently toss with a rubber spatula to coat (C).

A

B

C

Japanese Parfait with Fruit, Mochi, Agar-Agar Jelly, and Beans

(*Mitsumame*)

Equipment/Tools:
- Sieve
- Bowl
- 14 x 11 x 4.5 cm rectangular mold

Mitsumame brings back fond memories of my childhood in Japan when my mother used to take me out for this treat at the end of a fun shopping day. Here, I've created an easy version of the classic dessert using the Cook-Zen.

Makes 4 servings

Rice Dumplings:
100g shiratamako rice flour (see page 16)
90g plus 90g water

Syrup:
100g sugar
300g water
2 tablespoons Grand Marnier

Agar-Agar:
½ stick agar-agar (kanten)
250g water
30g sugar

Japanese Red Peas:
60g dried red peas (aka-endomame)
400g water
5g salt

200 to 250g fruit, cut into a ½-inch dice, for garnish (papaya, melon, pineapple, cherry, and other fruits in season, or canned fruit)

1 Set your microwave to a power level of 600 watts (see page 12 for more information).

2 To make the rice dumplings, in a bowl, combine the rice flour and 90g of water. Mix well, using your hands, until the dough is smooth and has the firmness of an earlobe.

3 Divide the dough into 12 pieces and roll each into a ball by hand. Make a thumb indentation in the middle to allow for even heat distribution and cooking.

4 Add 90g of water to the Cook-Zen. Close the lid and heat for 3 minutes with the steam holes set to "close." Open and place the shaped dough pieces in the Cook-Zen with the hot water. Close the lid and heat (at 600 watts) for 4 additional minutes with the steam holes set to "close." After cooking, rinse the dumplings under cold water. Drain and set aside in a bowl.

5 Rinse the Cook-Zen. To make the syrup, place 100g of sugar and 300g of water inside the Cook-Zen and stir. Close the lid and heat (at 600 watts) for 3 minutes with the steam holes set to "close." Add the Grand Marnier and stir to combine. Set aside and let cool.

6 To make the agar-agar jelly, tear the agar-agar into very small pieces by hand. Quickly rinse under cold water over a sieve and squeeze out excess water by hand.

7 Rinse the Cook-Zen, then place the agar-agar, 250g of water, and 30g of sugar inside. Cover and heat (at 600 watts) for 5 minutes with the steam holes set to "close." Whisk the mixture and, while still hot, strain it into a bowl using a sieve.

8 Pour the warm liquid into a jelly mold and let it set in the refrigerator until firm, about 20 minutes. Cut into ½-inch cubes.

9 Rinse the Cook-Zen. To prepare the red peas, wash and drain them, then place in the Cook-Zen with 400g of fresh water, cover with the lid and heat (at 600 watts) for 10 minutes with the steam holes set to "close." Add salt, mix, and let cool. Drain well.

10 To assemble the parfait, in 4 individual glass dessert bowls, arrange the dumplings, cubed agar-agar jelly, and the red peas. Pour 1 to 2 tablespoons of syrup over the ingredients and garnish with your favorite fruit toppings.

Japanese Arrowroot Jelly with Red Bean and Salted Cherry Blossoms

(*Kuzuzakura*)

Equipment/Tools:

- Whisk
- Bowl
- Sieve
- Wooden spatula
- 6 dome-shaped plastic *mizu-manju* molds or 2-ounce glass prep bowls

A

The subtle sweetness of arrowroot and red bean paste combined with salted cherry blossoms makes this *wagashi* a summer favorite. To make this recipe, you will need either plastic *mizu manju* molds or 2-ounce glass prep bowls.

Makes 6 servings

Red Bean Paste:
30g red bean powder
30g sugar
55g water

Arrowroot Jelly:
50g Japanese arrowroot starch powder (kuzuko)
200g water
80g sugar

6 salted cherry blossoms

1 Set your microwave to a power level of 600 watts (see page 12 for more information).

2 To make the red bean paste, mix together the red bean powder, 30g of sugar, and 55g of water in the Cook-Zen.

3 Close the lid and heat for 1 minute with the steam holes set to "close." After cooking, mix until the paste is combined. Divide into 6 equal portions, roll each into a ball, and set aside.

4 Rinse the Cook-Zen. To make the arrowroot jelly, whisk together the arrowroot powder and 200g of water in a bowl until smooth. Add 80g of sugar and mix. Strain the arrowroot liquid through a sieve into the Cook-Zen.

5 Cover with the lid and heat (at 600 watts) for 4 minutes with the steam holes set to "close."

6 After cooking, stir the mixture with a wooden spatula until it cools down and becomes opaque with a sticky consistency (A). Any white specks will dissolve as you stir the mixture.

7 Lightly rinse the cherry blossoms under cold water to remove any excess salt. Gently squeeze out excess water.

8 Place one blossom in the bottom of each mold.

9 With a wet spoon, scoop 1 tablespoonful of the cooked arrowroot mixture into the mold over the cherry blossom. Then place a red bean paste ball in the center and pour the arrowroot to the rim of the mold barely covering the red bean paste. Place in the refrigerator and let chill until set, about 20 minutes. Unmold the *manju* and serve cold.

Rice Flour and Arrowroot Dessert

(*Uiro*)

Equipment/Tools:

- Wooden spatula
- Bowl
- Whisk
- Sieve
- Cutting board
- Rolling pin
- Pastry brush
- Small cookie cutters

This traditional dessert is usually steamed for 20 to 25 minutes. With the Cook-Zen, it's ready in minutes. Enjoy cutting out fun and interesting shapes of your choice.

Makes about 15 to 20 pieces

Simple Syrup:
100g caster sugar
150g water

Dough:
25g arrowroot starch powder (kuzuko)
100g jyoshinko rice flour (see page 16)
150g water
1 scant drop red food coloring (optional)
Potato starch, for dusting

Red bean paste (see recipe on page 82) (optional)

1 Set your microwave to a power level of 600 watts (see page 12 for more information).

2 To make the simple syrup, combine the sugar and 150g of water in the Cook-Zen. Mix with a wooden spatula. Close the lid and heat for 4 minutes with the steam holes set to "close."

3 To make the dough, place the arrowroot powder and rice flour in a bowl and mix by hand, separating any clumps. Slowly add 150g of water and a scant drop of food coloring (leave the coloring out if you want the finished dessert to be white). Whisk until you get a smooth consistency (A). Add the simple syrup, then press and strain the mixture into the Cook-Zen using a sieve.

4 Close the lid and heat (at 600 watts) for 4 minutes with the steam holes set to "close." After cooking, mix with a wooden spatula (B).

5 Dust the cutting board with potato starch and when cool enough to handle, roll out the dough to about 1/8-inch thickness (C). Brush off any excess starch with a pastry brush and cut shapes out of the dough, using your favorite cookie cutters.

6 If desired, sandwich some red bean paste between two cutouts of dough.

RICE FLOUR AND PLANT-BASED STARCHES

Cinnamon Mochi
with Red Bean Paste
(*Nama Yatsuhashi*)

Equipment/Tools:
- Wooden spatula
- 2 bowls
- Whisk
- Cutting board
- Rolling pin
- Pastry brush
- Tea strainer

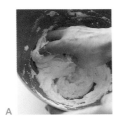

A

One of the most popular souvenirs from the city of Kyoto is the regional specialty, *yatsuhashi*. The nuanced bitterness of the cinnamon together with the sweet red bean paste is a perfect marriage of flavors. With the Cook-Zen, this sweet is easy to make at home.

Makes 8 to 10 pieces

Red Bean Paste:
30g red bean powder
30g sugar
55g water

Simple Syrup:
100g caster sugar
150g water

Dough:
10g shiratamako rice flour (see page 16)
25g arrowroot starch powder (kuzuko)
130g water
100g jyoshinko rice flour (see page 16)
Potato starch, for dusting

15g ground cinnamon
½ tablespoon powdered sugar

1 Set your microwave to a power level of 600 watts (see page 12 for more information).

2 To make the red bean paste, mix together the red bean powder, 30g of sugar, and 55g of water in the Cook-Zen. Close the lid and heat for 1 minute with the steam holes set to "close."

3 After cooking, mix with a wooden spatula until the paste is combined. Divide into 8 to 10 portions, form each into a ball, and set aside.

4 Rinse the Cook-Zen. To make the simple syrup, place 100g of sugar and 150g of water inside the Cook-Zen and stir. Close the lid and heat (at 600 watts) for 4 minutes with the steam holes set to "close." Stir the mixture.

5 To make the dough, mix the *shiratamako* rice flour, arrowroot powder, and 130g of water in a bowl by hand. Then add the *jyoshinko* rice flour and continue to mix by hand (A).

6 Add the dough mixture to the syrup in the Cook-Zen, whisking to combine. Close the lid and heat (at 600 watts) for 4 minutes with the steam holes set to "close."

7 Dust the cutting board with potato starch and roll out the dough to about ⅛-inch thickness. Cut into 3- x 3-inch squares and brush off any excess starch using a pastry brush.

8 Place a ball of red bean paste in the center of a dough square, and fold the dough over to make a triangle.

9 In a small bowl, mix the cinnamon and powdered sugar. Gently toss the triangular *mochi* in the cinnamon-sugar mixture. With a fine-mesh tea strainer, sprinkle with more cinnamon and sugar before serving.

Bracken Starch Mochi
with Roasted Soybean Flour
(*Warabi Mochi*)

Equipment/Tools:

- Wooden spatula
- Plate

When I was a child, *warabi mochi* was so commonly available that it was hard to appreciate. Now it brings back memories from my childhood and I get nostalgic just thinking about its soft texture. I often make this treat on a whim.

Makes 6 pieces

50g bracken starch (warabiko)
20g sugar
200g water
Roasted soybean flour (kinako), to taste
Japanese black sugar syrup (kuromitsu) (optional, see page 124
    for recipe)

1 Set your microwave to a power level of 600 watts (see page 12 for more information).

2 Combine the bracken starch, sugar, and water in the Cook-Zen. Mix until smooth. Close lid and heat for 2 ½ to 3 minutes with the steam holes set to "close."

3 After cooking, mix vigorously with a wooden spatula until the *mochi* becomes thick and cloudy. Let the *mochi* sit for a few minutes, until cool to the touch. Tear the *mochi* by hand into 6 pieces, place on a plate, and toss with the roasted soybean flour to coat.

4 If desired, drizzle some Japanese black sugar syrup over the *mochi* as a finishing touch.

Shiso Mochi Cake
(*Shiogama*)

Equipment/Tools:
- Bowl
- Tamis (Japanese-style drum sieve) or sieve
- 14 x 11 x 4.5cm rectangular mold
- Wax paper

A

B

C

This wagashi has a delicate flavor, lightly fragrant with *yukari* (a dried red shiso mix) and seasoned with a hint of salt. Making simple syrup can be tricky, but with the Cook-Zen it is simple indeed.

Makes one bar of mochi cake

Simple Syrup:
3 tablespoons potato starch syrup (mizuame)
50g hot water

180g sugar

250g kanbaiko rice flour (see page 17)
15g yukari (flavored dried red shiso mix)
5g salt

1 Set your microwave to a power level of 600 watts (see page 12 for more information).

2 To make the simple syrup, place the potato starch syrup and hot water in the Cook-Zen. Close the lid and heat for 2 minutes with the steam holes set to "close."

3 Place the sugar in a bowl and gradually mix in the simple syrup using your hands.

4 When the sugar and syrup mixture is combined, mix in the rice flour, yukari, and salt. Knead the mixture with the palm of your hand (A).

5 Press the mixture through a coarse-mesh tamis or sieve using a back-and-forth motion (B).

6 Cut two pieces of parchment paper to fit the mold. Line the mold with one piece of wax paper, then pour in the sifted semi-dry mixture, creating an even layer. Place another piece of wax paper on top and press down firmly with a flat-bottomed weight (C). When the mixture has set (about 15 minutes), cut into cubes or desired shapes.

Traditional
Tea Ceremony Sweets
(*Higashi*)

Equipment:
- Bowl
- Wooden or plastic *higashi* mold

Higashi are essential to the Japanese tea ceremony. I used to wonder how professionals made such beautiful pieces. With the Cook-Zen, the process is easier than I imagined. I've also discovered that these sweets keep well. Just be sure to store them in an airtight container in a cool, dry place.

Makes 30 pieces

Simple Syrup:
110g potato starch syrup (mizuame)
100g hot water

Scant drop of red or green food coloring (optional)
20g sugar
20g kanbaiko (rice flour, see page 17)
40g wasanbon (refined Japanese sugar, see page 15)

1 Set your microwave to a power level of 600 watts (see page 12 for more information).

2 To make the simple syrup, place the potato starch syrup and hot water in the Cook-Zen. Close the lid and heat for 2 to 3 minutes with the steam holes set to "close" (A). Weigh out 10g of this simple syrup and reserve the rest for another use (it will keep in the refrigerator for up to a week).

3 To make the sweets, combine 10g of simple syrup, and food coloring, if using, with 20g sugar in a bowl. Mix quickly and vigorously with your hands until the mixture comes together (B).

4 Add the *kanbaiko* (rice flour) to the simple syrup mixture and knead with the palm of your hand, pressing firmly (C).

5 Add the *wasanbon* (refined Japanese sugar) to the mixture (D), and lightly mix by hand. You'll notice the mixture becoming fluffier.

6 Fill the mold with the mixture, packing it in firmly with your hands. To unmold, remove the top layer of the mold and tap the corner of the mold to gently remove each *higashi*. Let them dry for 5 or 6 minutes after unmolding before storing in an air-tight container (E).

Cold Refreshing Wagashi

Agar-Agar

Wagashi are known to represent the seasons: spring, summer, autumn, and winter, each with its traditional offerings. The following *wagashi* recipes are made with gelatin and agar-agar jelly, ideal for hot summer days. They can be served chilled as desserts with afternoon tea.

Tri-Color Beans in White Curaçao Jelly

(*Seiryu*)

Equipment/Tools:

- Wooden spatula
- 12 x 7.5 x 4.5cm rectangular mold or 14-ounce glass bowl

A

B

The colorful, sweet candied beans in this *wagashi* represent pebbles in a cold, clear stream. You can use a bean jelly (*yokan*) mold or a glass bowl for a more appealing presentation.

Makes enough for 12 x 7.5 x 4.5cm mold

12g gelatin powder
200g water
75g sugar
1 tablespoon White Curaçao (orange liqueur)
150g red, green, and white sweet candied beans (amanatto), store-bought

1 Set your microwave to a power level of 600 watts (see page 12 for more information).

2 Mix the gelatin and water in the Cook-Zen. Close the lid and heat for 2 minutes with the steam holes set to "close" (A).

3 Add the sugar and the White Curaçao to the gelatin mixture. Mix well using a wooden spatula.

4 Gently fold the sweet beans into the gelatin mixture and pour into a mold or bowl (B). Chill in the refrigerator for over an hour, until firm.

Layered Red Bean Jelly
(*Azukiyose*)

Equipment/Tools:
- Wooden spatula
- 12 x 7.5 x 4.5cm rectangular mold

This simple recipe made with cooked sweet red beans and gelatin is the perfect dessert to have on a midsummer day while listening to wind chimes blowing in the wind.

Makes enough for a 12 x 7.5 x 4.5cm mold

100g water
5 to 6g gelatin powder
200g cooked sweetened red beans, store-bought

1 Set your microwave to a power level of 600 watts (see page 12 for more information).

2 Mix the water and gelatin powder in the Cook-Zen. Close the lid and heat for 1 ½ minutes with the steam holes set to "close."

3 Carefully fold the beans into the gelatin mixture using a wooden spatula. Pour into a mold and chill in the refrigerator for over an hour until firm.

Japanese Plum Wine Jelly

(*Umeshu Jelly*)

Equipment/Tools:
- 14 x 11 x 4.5cm rectangular mold

When I created this recipe I used plums preserved in a homemade seven-year-old plum wine, which gave the wagashi a beautiful amber hue. Plums from store-bought plum wine work well, too.

Makes enough for a 14 x 11 x 4.5cm mold

80g water
8g powdered gelatin
30g sugar
200g Japanese plum wine
½ tablespoon lemon juice
5 Japanese plums, preserved in plum wine

1 Set your microwave to a power level of 600 watts (see page 12 for more information).

2 Combine the water and gelatin in the Cook-Zen. Close the lid and heat for 1 ½ minutes with the steam holes set to "close."

3 Add the sugar, plum wine, and lemon juice to the gelatin mixture in the Cook-Zen and mix well.

4 Pit the plums and julienne the flesh. Add plums to the gelatin mixture, then slowly pour the mixture into the mold, being careful not to cause air bubbles in the jelly. Chill in the refrigerator for over an hour until set.

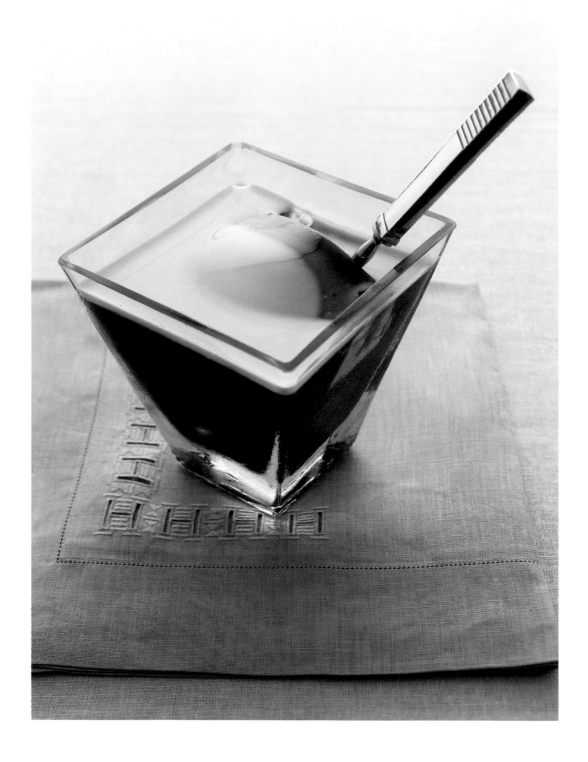

Japanese Black Sugar Jelly with Cream

(*Kurozato Jelly*)

Equipment/Tools:
- Wooden spatula
- 14 x 11 x 4.5cm rectangular mold or large glass bowl

This recipe is a simple dessert using only Japanese black sugar as the main flavoring ingredient. Japanese black sugar contains calcium and iron, among other minerals, that are said to be good for the body, especially for treating anemia.

Makes enough for one 14 x 11 x 4.5cm mold

230g raw Japanese black sugar (kurozatou)
200g plus 400g water
7.5g gelatin powder
Heavy cream, to taste

1 Set your microwave to a power level of 600 watts (see page 12 for more information).

2 Combine black sugar, 200g of water, and gelatin powder in the Cook-Zen and mix with a wooden spatula. Close the lid and heat for 2 to 3 minutes with the steam holes set to "close."

3 Once the sugar and gelatin have melted, add the remaining 400g of water to the mixture and stir thoroughly.

4 Pour the mixture into a rectangular mold or glass bowl and chill in the refrigerator for over an hour to set. Serve with heavy cream on top (do not whip).

Black Sesame Pudding

(*Goma Pudding*)

Equipment/Tools:

- Whisk
- Bowl
- 2 teacup-size dessert dishes

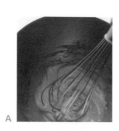

A

B

C

D

You can really taste the black sesame seeds in this *wagashi*. Chill the pudding in your favorite dessert dish before serving.

Makes 2 servings

5g gelatin powder
60g water
2 egg yolks
60g sugar
70g black sesame paste
100g whole milk
100g heavy cream

1 Set your microwave to a power level of 600 watts (see page 12 for more information).

2 Combine gelatin and water in the Cook-Zen. Close the lid and heat for 30 to 40 seconds with the steam holes set to "close."

3 In a bowl, whisk the egg yolks until smooth, then add the sugar. Whisk until well combined (A).

4 Slowly mix the sesame paste into the egg/sugar mixture (B), then gradually add the milk (C). Pour the mixture into the Cook-Zen, combining it with the gelatin, and mix well.

5 Close the lid and heat (at 600 watts) for 1 ½ to 2 minutes with the steam holes set to "close."

6 After heating, whisk until smooth. Let the mixture cool. When the mixture is just warm to the touch, add the heavy cream and whisk until combined (D). Pour into dessert dishes and chill in the refrigerator for over an hour until set.

Chilled Arrowroot Jelly with Red Bean

(*Mizu Manju*)

Equipment/Tools:

- Whisk
- Bowl
- 6 to 8 dome-shaped plastic *mizu manju* molds or 2-ounce glass prep bowls

This *wagashi* makes for a cool, refreshing treat any time of the year. The Cook-Zen eliminates the need for continuous stirring, making it easy to prepare this dish in 5 short minutes.

Makes 6 to 8 servings

Red Bean Paste:

40g red bean powder

40g sugar

80g water

30g powdered mizu manju mix, store-bought

60g sugar

200g water

3 to 4 teaspoons plum compote (see recipe on page 116), or store-bought fruit compote of your choice (optional)

1 Set your microwave to a power level of 600 watts (see page 12 for more information).

2 To make the red bean paste, mix together the red bean powder, 40g of sugar, and 80g of water in the Cook-Zen. Close the lid and heat for 1 ½ minutes with the steam holes set to "close." After cooking, mix until the paste is combined and set aside in a separate bowl.

3 Roll the bean paste into 6 to 8 balls, depending on how large you want them to be.

4 Rinse the Cook-Zen. Combine the *mizu manju* mix, 60g of sugar, and 200g of water in the Cook-Zen and whisk until smooth with no lumps.

5 Close the lid and heat (at 600 watts) for 5 minutes with the steam holes set to "close." Mix well after heating.

6 If using compote, place ½ teaspoon of it in the bottom of each mold.

7 Fill each mold about ⅓ of the way with the cooked *mizu manju* mixture, then place one bean paste ball in the middle of each mold or bowl. Top off with the *mizu manju* mixture until the bean paste is slightly covered and chill in the refrigerator for over an hour to set. To unmold, run the tip of a knife around the edge of the mold and carefully turn it over and unmold the dessert onto a plate.

Fresh-Water Buds in Wine Jelly

(*Junsai Wine Kan*)

Equipment/Tools:
- Bowl
- Sieve
- Whisk
- 8 jelly molds (each holding about 1 ½ ounces)

A

The buds of the water-shield plant (*junsai*) begin to appear in lakes in the early summer. Though the jelly sets easily at room temperature, it is best served chilled. This cool wine jelly melts in your mouth.

Makes 8 servings

½ stick agar-agar (kanten)
200g water
150g caster sugar
½ tablespoon potato starch syrup (mizuame)
50g white wine
8 tablespoons junsai, store-bought in bottles

1 Set your microwave to a power level of 600 watts (see page 12 for more information).

2 Tear the agar-agar into small pieces by hand and place in a sieve. Rinse under cold water and squeeze out any excess water.

3 Combine 200g of water and the rinsed agar-agar in the Cook-Zen. Close the lid and heat for 5 minutes with the steam holes set to "close." After cooking, strain the liquid into a bowl.

4 Return the agar-agar liquid to the Cook-Zen. Add the sugar and potato starch syrup. Close the lid and heat (at 600 watts) for 1 minute with the steam holes set to "close."

5 Uncover, whisk, add the wine, and whisk again.

6 Pour the mixture into the molds. Add a spoonful of *junsai* and let sit at room temperature or chill in the refrigerator for over an hour until set (A).

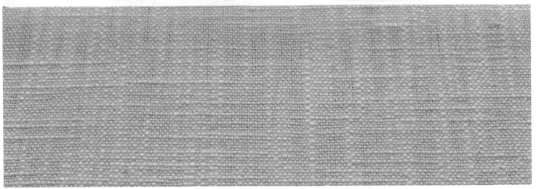

Colorful Agar-Agar Jelly *(Kingyoku)*

3 Variations:

Gourd-Shaped Agar-Agar Jelly (*Hyotan*)

Polka Dot Agar-Agar Jelly (*Mizutama Kingyoku*)

Colorful Marbled Agar-Agar Jelly Mix (*Irodori Kingyoku*)

Equipment/Tools:
- Sieve
- Bowl
- 15 x 13.5 x 4.5cm rectangular mold
- Cookie cutters, gourd-shaped or other shape of your choice

Gourd-Shaped Agar-Agar Jelly (*Hyotan*)

Agar-agar and potato starch syrup can be tricky ingredients to work with, as they tend to stick and burn when cooked over direct heat. With the Cook-Zen, it's a breeze. Be creative! Try using different colors and a variety of molds to make these beautiful, festive desserts.

Makes enough for one 15 x 13.5 x 4.5cm mold

½ stick agar-agar (kanten)
200g water
30g potato starch syrup (mizuame)
250g caster sugar
1 or 2 scant drops of green food coloring

1 Set your microwave to a power level of 600 watts (see page 12 for more information).

2 Tear the agar-agar into small pieces by hand over a sieve. Rinse under cold water and squeeze out any excess water.

3 In the Cook-Zen, combine the agar-agar and 200g of water. Close the lid and heat for 5 minutes with the steam holes set to "close." After cooking, strain the liquid into a bowl.

4 Pour the agar-agar liquid back in the Cook-Zen. Add the potato starch syrup, sugar, and food coloring, and mix well. Close the lid and heat (at 600 watts) for 4 to 5 minutes with the steam holes set to "close" (A).

5 Pour the liquid into the mold. Let it sit at room temperature for 2 hours or until set. Cut out desired shapes.

A

Equipment/Tools:

- Sieve
- Bowl
- 15 x 13.5 x 4.5cm rectangular mold
- Small ramekins
- Cocktail picks
- Round cookie cutters

Polka Dot Agar-Agar Jelly (*Mizutama Kingyoku*) and Colorful Marbled Agar-Agar Jelly Mix (*Irodori Kingyoku*)

Translucent agar-agar jelly is an ideal canvas to express your creativity. Polka dots and marble patterns, two of my favorite designs, are beautiful and simple to make with just some food coloring and cocktail picks.

Makes enough for one 15 x 13.5 x 4.5cm mold

½ stick agar-agar (kanten)
200g water
30g potato starch syrup (mizuame)
250g caster sugar
1 tablespoon Cointreau (optional)
Food coloring (green, red, yellow, blue), few scant drops each

1 Set your microwave to a power level of 600 watts (see page 12 for more information).

2 Tear the agar-agar into small pieces by hand and place in a sieve. Rinse under cold water, and then squeeze out the excess water.

3 Place 200g of water and agar-agar in the Cook-Zen. Cover and heat for 5 minutes with the steam holes set to "close." Strain the agar-agar liquid into a bowl.

4 Place the strained agar-agar liquid back into the Cook-Zen. Add the potato starch syrup and sugar. Whisk well. Cover and heat (at 600 watts) for 4 to 5 minutes with the steam holes set to "close." (Add Cointreau, if using.) Pour the hot agar-agar liquid into the mold.

5 Put a few drops of each food coloring into separate ramekins. You can also mix colors to make secondary colors (e.g., red + yellow = orange; green + yellow = yellow green; red + blue = purple).

A

B

To Make Polka Dots:

Let the agar-agar sit at room temperature for about 15 to 20 minutes, until it has begun to set. To test this, move the mold ever so gently. The agar-agar will appear to have a film on the surface. Dip the cocktail pick into the food coloring, then press the pick vertically down into the agar-agar to make a polka dot (A). Repeat with different colors. Let sit at room temperature for 2 hours or until set.

To Make a Marbled Pattern:

Let the agar-agar sit at room temperature for about 10 to 15 minutes, until it has just barely begun to set. Dip the cocktail pick into the food coloring. Press the pick vertically down into the agar-agar, then streak and swirl the color to create a marbled effect (B). Repeat with different colors. Let sit at room temperature for 2 hours or until set.

Agar-Agar Jelly à la Parisienne

I was invited to demonstrate *wagashi*-making at the famous Le Cordon Bleu Cooking School in Paris. For a bit of French flair, I added a tablespoon of Cointreau to the agar-agar jelly with multicolored polka dots. I cubed the jelly and served it in a beautiful glass serving-dish, giving this wagashi a whole new look and taste.

Agar-Agar Jelly with Fruit and White Curaçao

(*Fruit Kanten Yose*)

Equipment/ tools:

- Sieve
- Bowl
- Whisk
- Individual serving glasses

This refreshing dessert is made with fresh seasonal fruits, agar-agar jelly, and a splash of White Curaçao.

Makes 6 servings

½ stick agar-agar (kanten)
230g water
1 tablespoon potato starch syrup (mizuame)
120g sugar
1 tablespoon White Curaçao

200g raspberries
½ small melon, cubed or balled, into bite-size portions.
12 to 16 fresh cherries, pitted
80g blueberries

1 Set your microwave to a power level of 600 watts (see page 12 for more information).

2 In a bowl, tear the agar-agar into small pieces by hand and place in a sieve. Rinse under cold water and squeeze out any excess.

3 In the Cook-Zen, combine 230g water and agar-agar. Cover and heat for 5 minutes with the steam holes set to "close." Strain the liquid into a bowl.

4 Pour the strained agar-agar liquid back into the Cook-Zen and add the potato starch syrup and sugar. Whisk until well combined. Close the lid and heat (at 600 watts) for 2 minutes with the steam holes set to "close." After cooking, let it sit for about 10 minutes to cool.

5 Add the White Curaçao and mix well. Gently fold in the fruit.

6 Spoon the mixture into serving glasses and chill in the refrigerator for over an hour until set.*

* **Note:** You can also spoon the mixture into small ramekins lined with plastic wrap. Gather the ends of the plastic, twist to close, and tie with a bow to make little jelly "packages." Chill in the refrigerator for over an hour, unwrap and serve.

Agar-Agar Jelly with Mango and Cointreau
(*Mango Kanten Gelee*)

Equipment/Tools:
- Sieve
- 14 x 11 x 4.5 cm rectangular mold
- Food processor

A

B

Sweet fresh mangoes and a hint of Cointreau make this jelly a flavorful ending to any meal.

Makes 4 servings

¹/₃ stick agar-agar (kanten)
240g water
75g sugar
1 ripe mango (420 to 450g)
1 tablespoon lemon juice
1 tablespoon Cointreau

1 Set your microwave to a power level of 600 watts (see page 12 for more information).

2 Tear the agar-agar into small pieces by hand and place in a sieve. Rinse under cold water, then squeeze out any excess.

3 Combine the agar-agar and 240g of water in the Cook-Zen. Cover and heat for 5 minutes with the steam holes set to "close."

4 Add sugar to the agar-agar mixture and mix until the sugar completely dissolves. Strain the liquid into the mold and let it cool.

5 Peel and pit the mango. In a food processor, pulse the mango leaving a little bit of texture (A). Add lemon juice and Cointreau to the fruit, and lightly mix.

6 When the agar-agar has cooled off (but is not yet set), gently fold in the mango mixture (B). Do not over-mix. Chill in the refrigerator for over an hour until set.

- Japanese Plum Compote
  (Ume Amani)

- Chestnut Parfait
  (Mont Blanc aux Marrons)

- Japanese Sweet Potato and Red Bean Paste Roll
  (Satsumaimo Roll)

- Japanese Kabocha Squash with Coconut Sauce
  (Kabocha Coconut)

- Japanese Mugwort Leaf Cake with Japanese
  Black Sugar Syrup
  (Yomogi-fu Kuromitsu)

Seasonal Fruit and Vegetable Wagashi

Japanese Plums

Fruits and vegetables are traditional elements in Japanese sweets. They are often pureed and added to bean paste to flavor the *wagashi* or the dessert itself may be molded into the shape of the fruit or vegetable. Simple yet sophisticated Japanese aesthetics, along with attention to detail, have made *wagashi* culture what it is today.

The following recipes feature the flavors of particular fruits and vegetables. When selecting produce, try to use fresh seasonal ingredients at their peak of ripeness.

Japanese Plum Compote

(*Ume Amani*)

Equipment/Tools:

- Cooking chopsticks
- Bowl
- Sieve
- Air-tight glass jar or container

A

B

C

D

Use ripe plums if you can find them. Or, if you purchase green plums at the market, leave them on the counter for a few days until they turn golden yellow. This is one of my favorite recipes to serve at a dinner party. Please note that the compote requires a week to marinate before serving.

Makes 10 to 12 pieces

10 to 12 large ripe Japanese plums, each weighing about 40g
400g water
400g sugar

1 Set your microwave to a power level of 600 watts (see page 12 for more information).

2 Gently remove the stems from the plums by using a cocktail pick or the end of a chopstick (A).

3 Wash the plums, then place them in the Cook-Zen along with the water (B). Close the lid and heat for 5 to 6 minutes with the steam holes set to "close."

4 Leave the plums in the water, and let cool on the counter overnight in the Cook-Zen. Drain the plums well using a sieve, reserving the liquid if desired (see Note).

5 Place the plums in a sterilized, air-tight glass container. Add the sugar, cover, and let sit on the counter until the juice from the plums completely dissolves the sugar (this will take about a day). The compote will be ready to eat in about a week and will keep for years. If desired, chill the compote before serving.

* Note: The plum water (from step 4) makes for a refreshing drink. You can serve it as is or with shochu or brandy. It's great iced or at room temperature.

Chestnut Parfait

(Mont Blanc aux Marrons)

Equipment/Tools:

- Food processor
- Bowl
- Whisk
- Hand-held immersion mixer
- Individual serving glasses

A

B

C

This chestnut dessert is a real treat. I've added brandy for a touch of elegance, and I recommend this recipe to anyone who enjoys an occasional indulgence.

Makes 3 servings

Chestnut Paste:

100g sweetened chestnuts, store-bought (canned and peeled)
or homemade (see Note)
1 tablespoon brandy
100g heavy cream

Whipped Cream:

200g heavy cream
15g sugar

80g dark chocolate bar
3 whole boiled chestnuts, for garnish

1 Set your microwave to a power level of 600 watts (see page 12).

2 To make the chestnut paste, remove any thin skin from the canned chestnuts. Place them in a food processor and pulse a few times to break them up. Add the brandy and 100g of heavy cream and blend until smooth (A).

3 In a bowl, whip 200g of heavy cream and the sugar using a hand-held mixer until you get soft peaks. Set aside.

4 Grate the chocolate, using a knife, and place in the Cook-Zen. Close the lid and heat for 30 seconds with the steam holes set to "close." Stir with a whisk until the melted chocolate becomes smooth (B).

5 In a serving dish, spoon a few tablespoons each of whipped cream, chestnut paste, and chocolate, in this order. Make another set of layers, then garnish with a dollop of whipped cream and a whole chestnut.

* Note: If you are making sweetened chestnuts from scratch, take 10 to 12 whole, raw chestnuts and carefully make a slit along the side or top of the shell to prevent the chestnut from bursting when heated (C). Combine 200g of water with the chestnuts in the Cook-Zen and heat (at 600 watts) for 6 to 7 minutes with the steam holes set to "close." Remove the shells and the inner skin from the chestnuts. Blend the chestnuts in the food processor along with 30g of sugar.

Japanese Sweet Potato and Red Bean Paste Roll
(*Satsumaimo Roll*)

Equipment/Tools:

- Tamis (Japanese-style drum sieve)
- Wooden spatula
- Bowl
- Rolling pin
- 4 plastic freezer bags, 23 x 33cm (9" x 13")
- Plastic cling wrap
- Bamboo mat (makisu)

The contrasting colors of Japanese sweet potato and red bean paste make for a beautiful roll. You can also make an inside-out version by using the lighter-colored sweet potato for the outer layer.

Makes 2 rolls

Sweet Potato Paste:
1 Japanese sweet potato (about 250g)
15g butter
15g sugar
2 tablespoons heavy cream

Red Bean Paste:
100g red bean powder
100g sugar
240g water

1 Set your microwave to a power level of 600 watts (see page 12 for more information).

2 To make the Japanese sweet potato paste, wash the sweet potato (with the skin on) and place in the Cook-Zen. Cover and heat for 5 minutes with the steam holes set to "close." Check to see if the potato is thoroughly cooked by using a knife or skewer. It should easily pierce all the way to the center. If necessary, heat for an additional minute or two.

3 Peel the sweet potato and, while it is still hot, puree it by pressing it through a tamis and into a bowl. Add butter and 15g of sugar to the sweet potato and mix with a wooden spatula. When the paste has cooled, add heavy cream and mix.

4 Rinse the Cook-Zen. To make the red bean paste, combine the red bean powder, 100g of sugar, and water in the Cook-Zen, and mix well. Cover and heat (at 600 watts) for 3 minutes with the steam holes set to "close." After cooking, mix with a wooden spatula.

5 To make the roll, put half of each paste (sweet potato and red bean) into two separate plastic bags. Leave the bags open. Roll each out with a rolling pin to about ⅛-inch thickness. The red bean paste (for the outer layer) should be ¾ inch longer than the sweet potato paste. Reverse this order for an inside-out roll.

6 Cover the bamboo mat with plastic wrap. Cut the plastic bags and remove the pastes. First, place the red bean paste on the bamboo mat, followed by the sweet potato paste on top (reverse order if you want the sweet potato to be the outer layer). Be sure to align the two pastes at the bottom of the bamboo mat (the edge closest to you) and carefully start rolling (B). Gently remove the bamboo mat and plastic wrap. Repeat with remaining sweet potato paste and red bean paste. To serve, cut rolls into ¾-inch individual servings. Enjoy!

Japanese Kabocha Squash with Coconut Sauce

(*Kabocha Coconut*)

Equipment/Tools:
- Bowl
- Hand-held mixer

The texture of the kabocha comes out perfectly creamy when cooked in the Cook-Zen. Here, I've paired it with a coconut milk sauce, which enhances the natural sweetness of the squash.

Makes 4 servings

250g Japanese squash (kabocha)
100g heavy cream
40g sugar
60g coconut milk
Pinch of shredded coconut, for topping

1 Set your microwave to a power level of 600 watts (see page 12 for more information).

2 Seed the squash, then carefully cut into 1-inch cubes or bite-size portions. Place the squash in the Cook-Zen, cover, and heat for 5 minutes with the steam holes set to "close." Let cool. Then peel.

3 In a bowl, using a hand-held mixer, whisk the heavy cream and sugar until soft peaks form. Then gently fold in the coconut milk.

4 Place the cooked squash in a serving bowl or dish. Top with the coconut cream and a pinch of shredded coconut.

Japanese Mugwort Leaf Cake with Japanese Black Sugar Syrup

(*Yomogi-fu Kuromitsu*)

Equipment/Tools:
- Plate
- Small bowl

Nama-fu is a traditional Japanese delicacy based on highly refined wheat gluten that is combined with short-grained *mochi* rice flour, then, steamed. It is used in many savory, braised Japanese dishes and in classic tempura. This recipe calls for wheat gluten that has been flavored with mugwort leaves. I've combined it with Japanese black sugar syrup and a sprinkling of roasted soybean flour (*kinako*). This dessert is surprisingly delicious and quite unlike the traditional use of *nama-fu*.

Makes 5 to 6 servings

*1 package (120 to 150g) fresh or frozen mugwort-flavored
    wheat gluten (yomogi-fu)*
3 tablespoons water

For the Japanese Black Sugar Syrup:
60g Japanese black sugar powder
2 to 3 tablespoons water

Roasted soybean powder (kinako), for garnish

1 Set your microwave to a power level of 600 watts (see page 12 for more information).

2 Defrost the wheat gluten if you've bought it frozen. Slice into bite-size pieces and place in the Cook-Zen. Add 3 tablespoons of water, cover with the lid, and heat for 1 to 1 ½ minutes with the steam holes set to "close." Place the wheat gluten on a plate and let cool.

3 To make the black sugar syrup, combine the black sugar powder and 2 to 3 tablespoons of water in the Cook-Zen. Cover with the lid and heat (at 600 watts) for 2 to 3 minutes with the steam holes set to "close." Uncover and let cool.

4 Drizzle the sugar syrup on top of the wheat gluten and sprinkle with the roasted soybean powder to taste.

Beyond Wagashi

Making Sushi with Wagashi Molds

You can use your *wagashi* molds for more than just sweets. You can make beautiful "shaped sushi" (*oshizushi*) for any occasion. Here are some easy entertaining ideas.

Use the bean paste (*nerikiri*) molds in the chrysanthemum, cherry blossom, and plum-flower shapes to make these small sushi bites.

You'll need 400g of cooked sushi rice. You can color the sushi rice with a hardboiled egg yolk (passed through a sieve and folded into the rice) or add pink-colored sweet fish flakes (*sakura-denpun*) or chiffonade some shiso leaves to add green touches to the rice. Be creative! Fill the mold with sushi rice, making sure there are no air pockets. Gently remove the top of the mold and invert to unmold.

Sushi Tapas

Sushi tapas are easy to make. Prepare 400g of cooked sushi rice. Then place 30g of cooked rice, plain or flavored, into a push mold. Gently push the rice out of the mold onto a serving dish.

Top the shaped rice with your favorite sushi ingredients. Some popular toppings are tuna, snapper, raw or smoked salmon, and cooked shrimp. For roast beef sushi, cut thinly sliced roast beef into strips and wrap around the sushi rice. Garnish with wasabi.

Gift-Giving with Homemade Wagashi

Homemade Japanese sweets make delicious gifts for friends and family. Here are a few styling ideas to give your gifts a special touch.

Camellia Rice Cakes in a Bamboo Basket

Make sure there is enough space between each rice cake so that they do not stick together. Tie a camellia blossom to the basket with paper string or twine for a beautiful finish (the photo below is of a summer camellia bud).

Bean Paste Sweets in an Acrylic Jewelry Case

A transparent case is a wonderful way to showcase beautifully colored bean paste sweets. A two-tiered box makes for an especially gorgeous gift box. (You can find clear acrylic cases in stores such as The Container Store, www.containerstore.com.)

Shiso Mochi Cakes Wrapped in Gift Paper

Wagashi such as Shiso Mochi Cake and Traditional Tea Ceremony Sweets need to be protected from humidity. Wrap these sweets in wax or parchment paper, then finish wrapping them with gift paper of your choice, and tie a colorful linen string or ribbon around it to brighten things up.

Glutinous Rice Balls in a Bento Box

Packaging *mochi*-based desserts (*ohagi* and *dango*) in a bento box is ideal. Bento boxes made of natural materials such as Japanese cedar (*sugi*) are especially useful because they absorb just the right amount of moisture to keep the sweets fresh.

Source List for Wagashi Ingredients and Wagashi-Making Tools

Most *wagashi* ingredients are sourced from specialty stores and can be ordered online or purchased in-store. Make sure you have the correct measurements for a mold before ordering online.

In the US and UK:

Amazon
www.amazon.com
Cook-Zen pot, ingredients, and molds

Dainobu USA, Inc.
www.dainobu.us
36 West 56th St.,
New York, NY 10019
Tel: 212-707-8525
Ingredients

Kalustyan's
www.kalustyans.com
123 Lexington Ave.
New York, New York 10016
212-685-3451
Ingredients

Katagiri & Co., Inc.
www.katagiri.com
www.katagiristore.com
224 East 59th St.,
New York, NY 10022
Tel: 212-755-3566
Ingredients

Kinokuniya
www.kinokuniya.com
1073 Avenue of the Americas
New York, NY 10018
Tel: 212-869-1700
Stores nationwide: New York, New Jersey, Illinois, Washington, California, Oregon, Texas
Cook-Zen pot and molds

Mitsuwa Marketplace
www.mitsuwa.com
595 River Road
Edgewater, NJ 07020
Tel: 201-941-9113
Stores nationwide: New Jersey, Texas, and California: San Jose, San Diego, Santa Monica, San Gabriel, Costa Mesa, Irvine, and Torrance
Ingredients

Japan Centre
www.japancentre.com
19 Shaftsbury Avenue
London, W1D 7ED, England
Tel: +44-20-3405-1246
Ingredients

In Japan:

Tomizawa Shoten
www.tomiz.com
  Machida Flagship Store
  4-6-6 Haramachida
  Machida-Shi
  Tokyo, Japan 194-0013
  Tel: +81-42-722-3175
Specialty stores carrying 7,000 different dessert and baking ingredients; cooking utensils, and molds; red and white bean powders (Kanegiku-an and Shirogiku-an, made by Hakodate Nezuseian brand); catalogue and internet sales; 64 stores in Japan in Kanagawa, Chiba, and Saitama prefectures

Cuoca

www.cuoca.com

http://shop.cuoca.com/english

Jiyugaoka Flagship Store

Sweets Forest 1st floor

2-25-7 Midorigaoka, Meguro-ku,

Tokyo, Japan 152-0034

Tel: +81-3-5731-6200

Dessert ingredients (dairy products, chestnuts, squash, etc.); cooking utensils, and molds. Internet sales; 6 stores in Japan: Mitsukoshi Nihonbashi, Kichijyoji, Koshigaya (Saitama prefecture), Kyoto, and Takamatsu (Kagawa prefecture)

Araiwa Honten

www.araiwa.jp

2-6-10 Chuo, Aoba-ku

Sendai-shi, Miyagi-ken, Japan 980-0021

Tel: +81-22-222-5466

Culinary supplies (Cook-Zen pot, chopsticks, molds) and decorative products for gifts; phone and mail-order sales

Mantou

www.mantou.co.jp/proshop/index.html

1-4-2 Nishi-Asakusa, Taito-ku (store)

Tokyo, Japan 111-0035

Tel: +81-3-3842-2316

Fax: +81-3-3844-6686

Specialty wagashi ingredients for culinary professionals, but is open to the public; orders by phone or fax

Hakodate Nezuseian (company office)

Supplies bean paste (An) powder

Phone orders: +81-138-23-1952

Yokoyama

www.yokoyamacake.com

2-20-4 Nishi-Asakusa, Taito-ku (store)

Tokyo, Japan 111-0035

Tel: +81-3-3841-2300

Fax: +81-3-3841-4056

Wagashi tools and equipment, including custom-made wooden wagashi molds; catalogue and fax orders

Yoshida Kashi-dougu

www.kashidougu.com

2-6-5 Nishi-Asakusa, Taito-ku (store)

Tokyo, Japan 111-0035

Tel: +81-3-3841-3448

Fax: +81-3-3844-6417

Tools and equipment for making all kinds of desserts, not limited to wagashi; catalogue sales available

Ikesho Co, Ltd.

www.ikesho-global.ocnk.net

2 5 10 Narusegaoka

Machida

Tokyo 194-0011

Tel: +81-42-795-4311

Fax: +81-42-795-3431

Molds and kitchen tools

Index

S

Photography credits

Akio Sekine: 20, 21, 28, 29, 35, 38, 42, 43 (A, B, C), 47, 89 (A, B, C, D), 126, 127

Tatsuya Inou: 109

Shoji Shirane: 9, 14, 16, 17, 22, 25, 25, 27, 30, 31, 32, 33, 34, 36, 37, 39, 40, 41, 43 (D), 44, 45, 48 (A), 49, 50, 52, 55, 57, 59, 60, 61, 64, 65, 66, 67, 69, 71, 72, 73, 74, 75, 77, 79, 78, 80, 81, 82, 83, 84, 86 (A, B, C), 87, 88, 89 (E), 91, 92, 93, 94, 97, 98, 100, 101, 102, 103, 104, 105, 106, 107, 109, 110, 112, 113, 115, 116, 117, 118, 119, 120, 121, 122, 125, 128

Cover photo: Shoji Shirane
Author photo: Tina Rupp